Excel 2022

Learn From Scratch Any Fundamentals, Features, Formulas, & Charts by Studying 5 Minutes Daily | Become a Pro Thanks to This Microsoft Excel Bible with Step-by-Step Illustrated Instruction

By Georgie Howell

Table of Contents

Introduction

Before attending a job interview, you should have a solid understanding of Microsoft Excel. Everyone utilizes Microsoft Excel, from economists to cashiers to department heads. It is not restricted to large organizations; small company owners and youths utilize it daily. Consequently, it is something you cannot neglect. Understanding basic Excel operations (at least a handful) is required for employment in the modern context. Several alternative spreadsheet tools are available, but Excel is likely the most used. People have utilized it over the previous three decades, and it has acquired numerous new features throughout time. Excel's biggest strength is its vast range of business applications, such as accounting, database administration, forecasting, research, inventory and payment tracking, and business analytics. You may have used Excel in school to populate several number tables or to add new cells. Excel, on the other hand, is far more difficult. Did you notice, for example, that the application is capable of all of the following:

- ❖ Graphs and charts
- ❖ Text Manipulation
- ❖ Tasks are automated
- ❖ Data Storage and Import
- ❖ Dashboards/Templates
- ❖ Crunching the numbers
- ❖ Organize data in a user-friendly manner.
- ❖ So you don't have to do basic and difficult mathematical functions.
- ❖ Convert large amounts of information into visually appealing graphical representations.
- ❖ Evaluate the data and generate forecasts for the future.
- ❖ Generate, modify, and recreate pixelated graphics

There appears to be much more to this application than you realize, and you can use it in any circumstance. It is less about columns of data and more about how quickly and effectively it solves numerous complex problems. This shift in perspective will enable you to comprehend how Excel may assist.

Chapter 1: - Excel Basics

Microsoft Excel is a useful and effective tool for data processing and analysis. It is a database application containing numerous columns and rows; each intersection is referred to as a "cell." Each cell holds a single piece of information or data. By arranging the data in this style, you may quickly discover specifics and extract information from changing data.

Excel is a Microsoft spreadsheet-based software tool that coordinates data and documents using formulae and functions. Companies of various sorts use Excel analysis all around the globe to do financial analysis.

Microsoft will release two versions of Office: a consumer edition called Office 2022 and a business version called Office LTSC. Office 2022 will be released later this year for Windows and macOS, and it is aimed at those who do not want to commit to the cloud-based Microsoft 365 versions. It is similar to the recent Office 2019 release.

Although the Office LTSC (Long-Term Servicing Channel) edition would contain accessibility improvements, dark mode support, and Excel capabilities, like Dynamic Arrays and XLOOKUP, Microsoft has not announced all Office 2022's changes and updates yet. Office 2022 will have similar features.

There will not be any big UI changes here, either. The most visible change is dark mode, but Microsoft will focus on the Microsoft 365 editions of Office, which will include most of the UI and cloud-based features.

Microsoft's Office LTSC, on the other hand, is a clear admission that not all business customers can transition to the cloud. "It's a matter of struggling to meet people at their place," says Jared Spataro, the president of Microsoft 365, in the interview with

Verge. "In the previous ten months, we've seen a significant increase in customers who have moved to the cloud. At the same time, we have customers that feel they should not move to the cloud because of their unique circumstances."

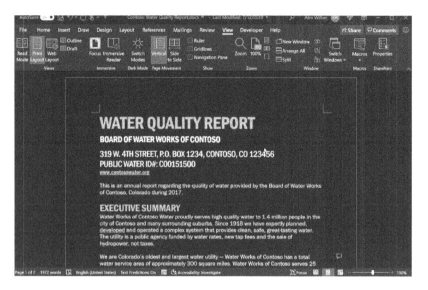

Those instances include organizations where processes and applications cannot be altered monthly or factories that rely on Office and need a set time-release. Microsoft has committed to a possible permanent version of Office, albeit the pricing and service for new models will be changed.

Office LTSC will also be financed for just five years, rather than the typical seven years provided by Microsoft. Office Professional Plus, Office Standard, and individual apps will all face a 10% price hike in Office 2022, but a user and small business costs will remain stable.

As a result, the Office LTSC support time is more accurately aligned with Windows, and Microsoft is harmonizing both Office and Windows update schedules. The following Office LTSC and Windows 10 LTSC versions will be released in the second half of 2022. "They'd be closely synchronized," Spataro adds, "but we don't have the details for the Windows release yet." "The goal is to bring them together so that enterprises can deploy and manage them in a coordinated manner."

Microsoft now aims to deliver an Office LTSC trial in April, with a full release later this year. The consumer Office 2022 version, on the other hand, would not be included in the preview. OneNote would be included in the 32-bit and 64-bit versions of the current Office editions.

How is Microsoft Excel Used?

Excel is a popular tool for data management and financial reporting. It may be found in both corporate roles and small companies.

Some of Excel's most common uses are as follows:

- Accounting
- Data entry
- Financial reporting
- Data maintenance
- Charting and graphing
- Programming
- Time management
- Task management
- Financial modeling
- Customer relationship management (CRM)

Microsoft Excel's History

Everyone who has worked in an office or attended school in the past three decades is familiar with Microsoft Excel. However, if you've been doing it for a while, you're aware that it's not as popular as rivals.

Microsoft published Excel as the second spreadsheet application, following Multiplan for CP/M OS devices. Unfortunately, its immediate opponent, Lotus 1-2-3, was a "killer app."

According to Merriam-Webster, a programming result of such great relevance or renown that it guarantees the efficacy of the linked technology. The IBM PC and its variants were the most successful computers of the 1980s, thanks in part to the popularity of Lotus 1-2-3. In the 1990s, IBM's purchase of Lotus Creation was not unexpected.

Microsoft released (Excel 1.0) in 1985 for Apple Macintosh? Microsoft did not distribute Excel 2.0 for MS-DOS until 1987. (In reality, Excel was bundled with Windows 2.0, and it consumed all of the RAM in the office system!) Excel and Lotus 1-2-3 will battle during the next several years.

```
 4  Owner's Funds                              $35,000.00
 5  Bank Loan                                   60,000.00
 6                                            ------------
 7   Total Cash Available                                    $95,000.00
 8                                                           ============
 9 Organizational & Pre-Operating Expenses
10  Advertising for Opening                     $1,250.00
11  Deposits-Phone & Utilities                   1,167.00
12  Decorating & Remodeling                      4,500.00
13  Fixtures & Equipment                         2,500.00
14  Licenses & Permits                             275.00
15  Professional Fees                            1,800.00
16  Rent-2 months security+1 month rent          2,925.00
17  Other Expenses                               1,500.00
18                                            ------------
19   Total Org'l & Pre-Operating Expenses                    15,917.00
20                                                           ------------
```

Microsoft Office was launched in November of 1990. The package's first edition includes PowerPoint 2.0, Word (1.1), and Excel (2.0). According to the October 1, 1990 issue of Information World, "all three applications contain support for Data Dynamic Exchange (DDE), which enables programs to transfer data using Windows resources in near real-time." This suggests that the three applications will communicate with one another, allowing the creation of a digital office.

When looking for a device, many individuals ask whether the hardware will aid in their planning or wind up in the trash. Microsoft released Windows (3.1) in 1992, with enhanced graphical usability and a new file system interface, Program Manager.

Therefore, it is not surprising that almost soon after its release, it became the most popular operating system for IBM PCs. Offices were among the earliest adopters of Windows since it was and would remain compatible with their existing software. Microsoft Office was compatible with all major computer platforms, but was exclusively offered to Mac users (OS). However, during the early 1990s Apple's business image eroded..

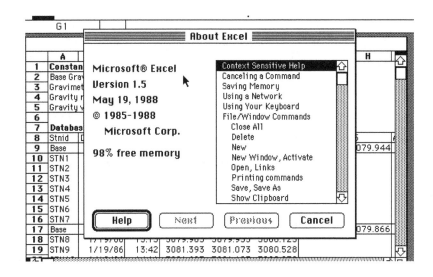

Excel had been updated four times when Windows 95 and Excel 95 were released. This had already overtaken Lotus (1-2-3), likewise having trouble adjusting to Windows' capability.

At the time, IBM was seeking to offer a Windows-based application software program called Lotus SmartSuite. Lotus 1-2-3 was also recommended for IBM's operating system (OS/2). Consequently, Microsoft refused to let IBM's manufacturing division pre-install Windows 95 on retail PCs until just before its release.

IBM's Lotus (SmartSuite) failed to endure a decade despite being one of the first genuinely killer games. Microsoft Office also contains Access, Outlook, Publisher, Skype and the other three services.

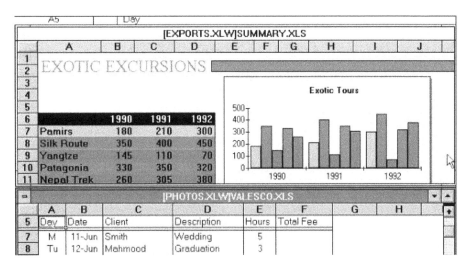

They gained knowledge from the first time Lotus annihilated Multiplan, primarily regarding the market. It paves the way for the creation of a killer app package that would aid enterprises worldwide. This led them down the path of developing a formidable operating system foundation to tie everything together. Due to earlier economic failures, Microsoft has transformed the business practices of society.

Data Functions, Formulas, and Shortcuts

There are numerous tools, algorithms, and keyboard shortcuts that can be used to increase Excel's utility.

Finance and Accounting Applications

Excel is frequently utilized in the banking and accounting sectors. Numerous businesses rely only on Excel spreadsheets for budgeting, planning, and accounting purposes. Even though Excel is a "information" processing technology, financial data is the most commonly processed data type.

Excel is the most powerful financial program accessible, per CFI. Excel's greatest advantages are its robustness and accessibility, despite the fact that most financial applications are designed to do complex tasks. Excel templates for analysts should be as efficient as feasible. Excel is utilized by accountants, investment managers, analysts, and experts in a variety of financial fields in their everyday job.

Chapter 2: - Why Learn Excel 2022?

In this chapter, you will go through why to learn Excel formulas and some of the basic Excel formulas in an excel spreadsheet.

Why Use Formulas?

This list is for you if you have ever questioned whether it is beneficial to spend time learning Excel formulae. Your expertise with formulas may aid you in various ways since they are the glue that holds spreadsheets together across the globe.

If you've ever considered whether it's worth your time to learn Excel formulae, this list can help you decide.

Because formulas are at the core of spreadsheets, becoming proficient in their use may benefit you in various contexts. Here are 10 motives why you should make it a priority to improve your familiarity with formulae, which you can read about below.

1. Formulas are essential for many different types of work. Over ninety percent of respondents regarding formulae said Excel formulas were "essential," "extremely important," or "critical" to the performance of their work duties.

2. Formulas are an effective tool for documenting and storing a solution that is currently in use (examples). They allow you to redo the answer anytime you choose and do it with pinpoint precision every time. They are a significant improvement over your poor memory.

3. Formulas are a useful tool for bringing your ideas into the actual world. Have you ever had the experience when you can describe what you need to achieve in simple English, but you've no clue how to accomplish it in Excel? You can construct the analysis that is in your thoughts using formulas.

4. Your familiarity with mathematical formulae enables you to create more effective spreadsheets. You can arrange data in a manner that makes use of formulae, which significantly decreases the number of mistakes and the amount of troubleshooting required. (To be honest, Pivot Tables also assist you in accomplishing the same goal.)

5. Since very few people are proficient with Excel formulae, having proficiency in this area is an opportunity to put oneself at a distance from the race by

delivering more value and being more productive. And productivity is something that every company strives for.

6. If you are skilled with formulae, you will be able to construct beautiful solutions that do not involve a lot of intricacies. There is nothing in Excel that is more harmful than needless complexity since it makes it hard to comprehend whether a spreadsheet is truly running well or not.

7. Because choices in the corporate world are often made using spreadsheets, having a strong understanding of formulae allows you to be close to your action.

8. Formulas let you easily visualize facts. When you use formulae alongside conditional formatting, you can "see" significant patterns, insights, and correlations instantly.

9. If you're good with formulae, you'll have a whole set of razor-sharp tools at your disposal while trying to solve difficulties. Without formula expertise, you are compelled to employ a dull saw for every work, regardless of how lengthy or repetitive it may be.

10. Formulas allow you to go home on time. If you can complete your task more quickly and have more time to spend with your friends and family, you should learn how to apply formulae. Priceless.

How to Add Text to a Cell in Excel?

Once you have mastered the process of entering data into an Excel spreadsheet, creating data tables won't take as much time as before.

If you haven't been told how to input data before, it may be a bit difficult; thus, you must stick to the guidelines below to discover the tips and tricks for simply entering your data into your spreadsheet.

Entering data in Excel worksheet

Cells in a worksheet may have either a value (such as a number or date) or a label (which can be either text or another cell's label).

First, you'll need to move your cell pointer to the desired location before you can begin entering data. As you enter data, you'll see it on the worksheet (within the example below, text displays in cell A 1) and into your Formula Bar.

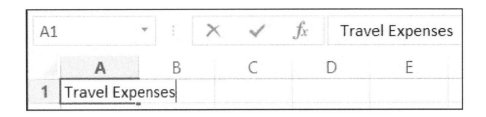

2. Enter the information into the field and press the ENTER key. When you click on a cell, the next accessible cell below will become the active one.

By pressing ESC instead of enter, you can prevent data from being entered into a cell.

Deleting & replacing data

To remove information from a cell, click on the cell and then hit the DELETE key.

Simply overwrite the contents of a cell with new text to replace it. The old information will be deleted when the new information is in place.

Using Undo & Redo

Sometimes, you may input information to realize that you messed it up.

Most of the time, you wish you could return to your position before committing the error. Don't worry if this occurs; click the "Undo" button to undo your most recent action.

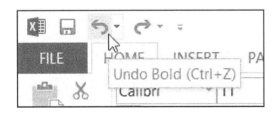

You can keep pressing it until you reach a point where you once again feel like you are in control of the situation.

You also can click the "Redo" button if you make a mistake that causes you to go back more than one step. These buttons are amazing, and I see that you use them often.

Overlapping data

When you put data into a too wide column for the data you entered, it will spill over into the following column. The word "Travel Expenses" is placed into cell A1 in the example that can be seen below; nonetheless, it gives the impression that the content is contained in cell B1. When you choose cell A1 and look at the Formula bar, you can see that both letters are in that cell.

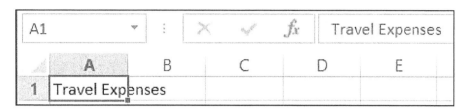

You are free to keep the content if you do not intend to use the column it is extending since it overlaps. However, as quickly as you insert text into the cell overlapped, it will seem as if your content has been lost. This effect will remain until you remove one of the overlapping cells. The phrase "Amount exclusive of GST" has been inserted into cell C3 of the example that can be seen below. However, a portion of the information in cell C3 is obscured by the contents of cell D3.

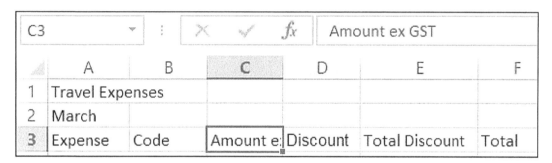

When cell C3 is selected, the Formula Bar updates to display the selected cell's contents. The width of column C must be modified so that the whole text of cell C 3 may be seen at once.

Excel Multiplication Formula

Since multiplying data is one of the operations used the most in Excel, the fact that there are multiple methods to do this task should not surprise anybody.

You are free to use whatever way while working with your spreadsheet on either a Mac or a PC will allow you to achieve the goals you have set for yourself.

The following are some of the most straightforward approaches to multiplying numbers:

Instructions for multiplying in Excel

This may be achieved quickly & easily by utilizing a simple formula to multiply values in a single cell.

If you enter "=2*6" into the cell and hit Enter, the cell should update to show the number 12.

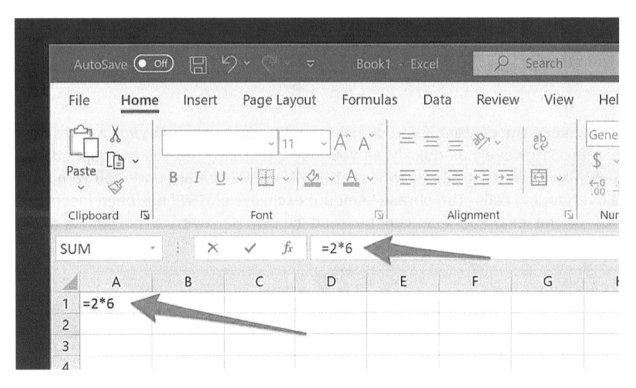

Utilizing the star as a multiplicator is the most straightforward method.

In addition, you may multiply the contents of two distinct cells together.

1. In one of the cells, enter "=."

2. Navigate to the cell that houses the first value you would like to multiply and click there.

3. Type "*".

4. Select the second cell you want to multiply by clicking on it.

5. Hit Enter.

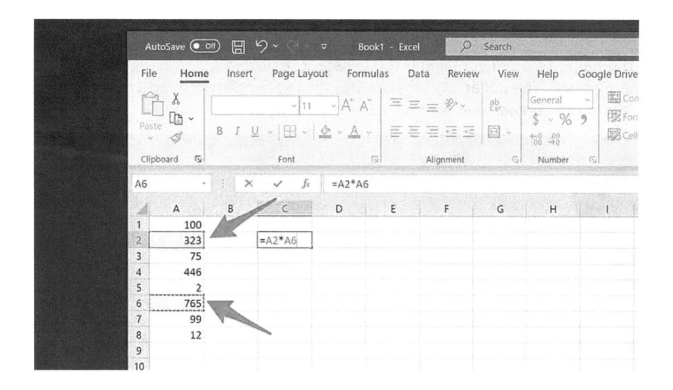

By clicking on the cells, you may reference them in a multiplication formula.

How to multiply numbers & cells using the PRODUCT formula

When utilizing the PRODUCT formula, you are not restricted to multiplying only two cells at once; rather, you may multiply anywhere from two to 255 values simultaneously.

You can multiply individual cells and integers using this formula by splitting them with commas, & you can multiply a sequence of cells using a colon.

For instance, the formula "= PRODUCT (A 1, A 3: A 5, B 1, 10)" instructs Excel to do the multiplication (A 1 x A 3 x A 4 x A 5 x B 1 x 10) since the A 3: A 5 instruction instructs Excel to perform the multiplication on A 3, A 4, and A 5.

Keep in mind that the order in which these cells & numbers are entered does not affect the multiplication result.

The formula for multiplying a column of numbers by a fixed number

Suppose you need to multiply a set of integers by the same factor. A direct reference to a cell containing the constant is all that's needed to do this.

The first step is to arrange the numbers to be multiplied into a column and then enter the constant into a separate cell.

Simply select the first cell to be multiplied, then write "=" in a new cell.

Input the name of a cell containing the constant, followed by a "$" before the letter and the number. The dollar sign makes this an exact reference, so you can copy & paste it into the spreadsheet without worrying about any changes.

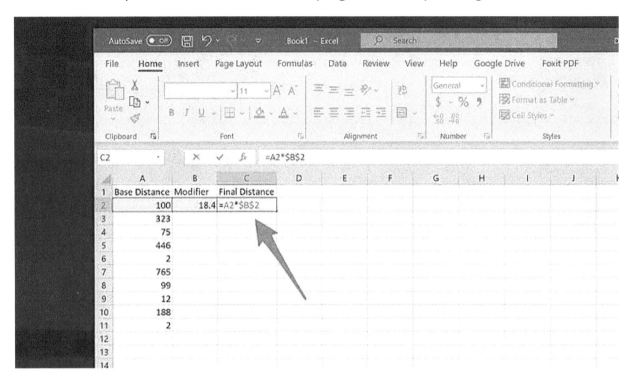

It's easy to refer to specific cells inside a formula using the $ symbol.

4. Hit Enter.

5. You may now execute the multiplication on either number by copying and pasting what you have just seen into other cells. Drag it by its bottom right corner to replicate a cell, as described in the previous sentence. This is the simplest method.

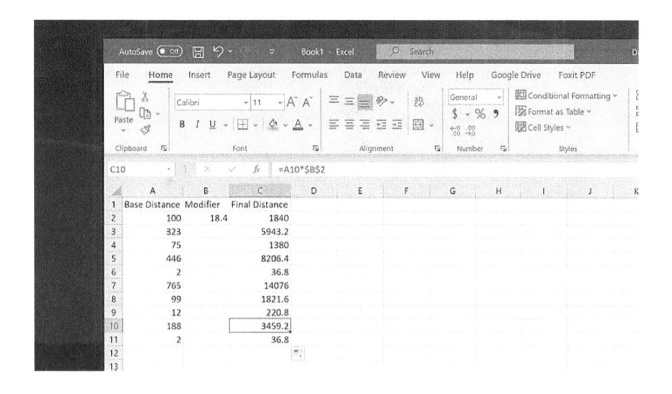

IF Function of Excel

The IF function is a check function that returns one value depending on whether a statement is true. However, it returns a different value depending on whether a statement is false. You can compare a value to your forecast throughout the functionality.

The following values may be sent into the IF function to be evaluated.

=IF (Logical_text, [Value_if_true], [Value_if_false])

- The value or logical expression that must be assessed and categorized as TRUE or FALSE is called "logical text" (Required Argument).

- (Probable Defense) Value if correct This value will be shown after the reasonable assessment if it is found to be TRUE.

- If the rational evaluation generates a FALSE result, the value of false (Possible Argument) will be returned.

To perform this function, the following logical operators may be utilized:

Equal to (=)
Greater than (>)
Greater than or equal to (≥)
Less than (<)
Less than or equal to (≤)
Not equal (≠)

Check to verify that the number in the A2 cell is more than 500. =IF (Yes" and "No"; A2>500)

| SEARCH | ▾ | : | × | ✓ | fx | =IF(A2>500,"Yes","No") |

⋅	A	B	C	D	E	F	G
1	Price	Result					
2	400	=IF(A2>500,"Yes", "No")					
3	800	IF(logical_test, [value_if_true], [value_if_false])					
4		212					
5		454					
6		789					

Stick to the steps in the preceding section to determine the values of A3 through B6: A3 must be more than 500, "Yes," "No," A4 must be greater than 500, "Yes," "No," A5 must be greater than 500, and A6 must be greater than 500, "Yes," "No."

| C13 | ▾ | : | ⅄ | ✓ | fx |

⋅	A	B	C	D
1	Price	Result		
2	400	No		
3	800	Yes		
4	212	No		
5	454	No		
6	789	Yes		

Excel Array Formula

You can conduct several computations all at once with the assistance of an array formula, or it can conduct one or more computations an unlimited number of times inside a certain cell range.

In these formulae, the referenced values might occur in the form of values inside a row, inside a column, or within a matrix (columns & rows). It is much simpler to present some instances to provide a more in-depth explanation of the array formula.

20

Without your Array Formula

You may see a variety of fruits listed in the illustration below (A2: A9), together with the quantity sold each day (B2: B9) & price per item (C2: C9). Within every revenue column cell, the revenue for each fruit is computed (D2: D9). Using a formula for multi-cell arrays will allow you to do this task more quickly.

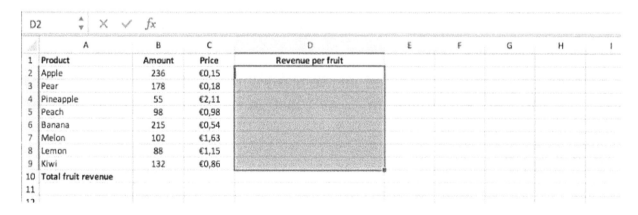

Multi Cells Array Formula

Using just one formula, the multi cells array formula would yield various outcomes that may be found anywhere inside a column or row. To calculate all the values of the column labeled "Revenue per fruit" at the same time in the example that was just shown, you begin by choosing the cell range inside which you wish to publish the results, and then you hit the F2 key to choose the first cell within range:

After that, you put the following formula into the chosen cell D2 of the array:

	SUM		×	✓	fx	=B2:B9*C2:C9					

	A	B	C	D	E	F	G	H	I
1	Product	Amount	Price	Revenue per fruit					
2	Apple	236	€0,15	=B2:B9*C2:C9					
3	Pear	178	€0,18						
4	Pineapple	55	€2,11						
5	Peach	98	€0,98						
6	Banana	215	€0,54						
7	Melon	102	€1,63						
8	Lemon	88	€1,15						
9	Kiwi	132	€0,86						
10	Total fruit revenue								
11									
12									

BUT STOP WHAT YOU'RE DOING! After you have finished creating the formula, pressing the "Enter" key will cause Excel to solely compute the outcome of the current row. This formula is identified as a CSE formula, and the reason for this is that it can only run properly when the keys CTRL, SHIFT, and ENTER are pressed simultaneously.

	D2		×	✓	fx	{=B2:B9*C2:C9}					

	A	B	C	D	E	F	G	H	I
1	Product	Amount	Price	Revenue per fruit					
2	Apple	236	€0,15	€35,40					
3	Pear	178	€0,18	€32,04					
4	Pineapple	55	€2,11	€116,05					
5	Peach	98	€0,98	€96,04					
6	Banana	215	€0,54	€116,10					
7	Melon	102	€1,63	€166,26					
8	Lemon	88	€1,15	€101,20					
9	Kiwi	132	€0,86	€113,52					
10	Total fruit revenue								
11									
12									

As can be seen, the formula computed all the array's values at the same time. Excel indicated that the calculation was an array function by adding brackets {} in the appropriate places around it.

Single Cell Array Formula

The formula for an individual cell array will only yield one result inside that cell, even though it may execute one or more computations.

In this example, your total income from the fruit may, of course, be determined by using a SUM function to the numbers that are found in the column labeled "Revenue per fruit":

D10 | × ✓ | fx | =SUM(D2:D9)

	A	B	C	D	E	F	G	H	I
1	Product	Amount	Price	Revenue per fruit					
2	Apple	236	€0,15	€35,40					
3	Pear	178	€0,18	€32,04					
4	Pineapple	55	€2,11	€116,05					
5	Peach	98	€0,98	€96,04					
6	Banana	215	€0,54	€116,10					
7	Melon	102	€1,63	€166,26					
8	Lemon	88	€1,15	€101,20					
9	Kiwi	132	€0,86	€113,52					
10	Total fruit revenue			€776,61					
11									
12									

In contrast, while using your array function, you may skip through the intermediate sums without impacting the final tally. You choose the cell where you wish to share the sum of fruit sales and input the formula =SUM (B2: B9 * C2: C9):

SUM | × ✓ | fx | =SUM(B2:B9*C2:C9)

	A	B	C	D	E	F	G	H	I
1	Product	Amount	Price	Revenue per fruit					
2	Apple	236	€0,15						
3	Pear	178	€0,18						
4	Pineapple	55	€2,11						
5	Peach	98	€0,98						
6	Banana	215	€0,54						
7	Melon	102	€1,63						
8	Lemon	88	€1,15						
9	Kiwi	132	€0,86						
10	Total fruit revenue			=SUM(B2:B9*C2:C9)					
11									
12									

To see the outcomes, use CTRL + SHIFT + ENTER once again. By just hitting Enter, you will trigger the '#VALUE!' error typical of Excel. After successfully running the array function, the sum will be shown in the corresponding cell, and brackets will once again surround the starting formula to indicate that it pertains to an array formula.

D10 | × ✓ | fx | {=SUM(B2:B9*C2:C9)}

	A	B	C	D	E	F	G	H	I
1	Product	Amount	Price	Revenue per fruit					
2	Apple	236	€0,15						
3	Pear	178	€0,18						
4	Pineapple	55	€2,11						
5	Peach	98	€0,98						
6	Banana	215	€0,54						
7	Melon	102	€1,63						
8	Lemon	88	€1,15						
9	Kiwi	132	€0,86						
10	Total fruit revenue			€776,61					
11									
12									

Functions that work with arrays may be risky.

Array functions are something that you see as potentially risky since they make collaboration inside a single spreadsheet very mistake prone. It's possible that your colleague is not acquainted with array methods and accidentally changed anything without using CTRL+SHIFT+ENTER.

Average Formulas in Excel

Using the AVERAGE function, you will understand the information well, such as the average number of owners in a certain shareholding pool.

=AVERAGE (number 1, [number 2], …)

Example:

=AVERAGE (B 2: B 11) – Shows the simple average, like (SUM (B 2: B 11)/10)

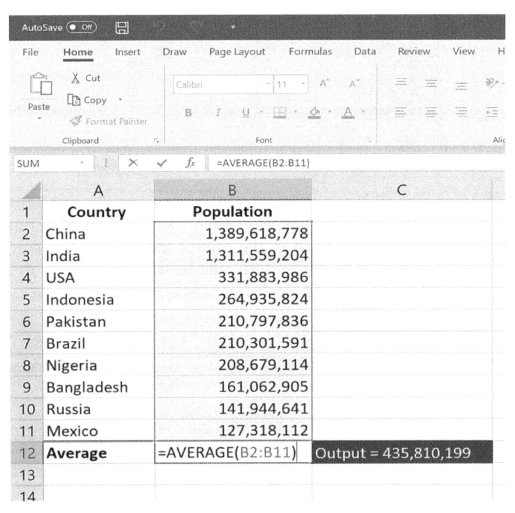

Percentage Formula in Excel

A figure expressed as a fraction of one hundred is referred to as a percentage. The notation for a percentage is a percent sign, which is written after a number. For instance, the notation for ten percent, sometimes known as 10%, is represented as 10/100. There are no units associated with the percentage.

Calculations were simplified thanks to the percentage that was provided. It may be tricky to precisely portray a part transgression, such as one-twelfth, two-thirds, etc., in written form. However, converting the fraction into a percentage is a simple process. As a result, the % is used in many aspects of your day-to-day lives.

For instance, the value of the fraction 2/5th expressed as a % is expressed as 2/5 multiplied by 100, which is 40%.

Percentage Formulas

Calculations may be made using an equation known as a formula. The computations conducted by humans are neither precise nor speedy. Excel's calculating process is quite comparable to that of a calculator. The following is a discussion of the percentage formulas:

Profit percentage = Sale price - actual price / actual price x 100

Or

Profit percentage = (Sale price / cost price- 1) x100

The distinction between the retail price and the cost price of a product is known as the "selling price," and it is the cost for which the item is sold to customers. The profit percentage is the amount of money made from selling your product.

Loss percentage = Actual price - sale price / Actual price x 100

Or

Profit percentage = (1 - Sale price / Actual price) x 100

When the selling price is lower than the cost price, this results in a loss for the business. It indicates that the seller sold the item at prices that were lower than the price at which they originally acquired the item.

To calculate the loss percentage, you may also apply the profit percentage method. The essential distinction is that it will be expressed in negative form.

Difference percentage = (B / A - 1) X 100

Where A & B refer to the goods for which the percentage of the difference between them must be determined.

Average percentage = Sum of all commodities / Number of the commodities x 100

The sum of each commodity's price, divided by the total number of prices, is how the average price is arrived at. In other contexts, you could refer to it as an average.

First, let's talk over some of Excel's most prevalent functions.

Data Sorting

Excel makes it quite simple for you to sort the data with only a few clicks.

Built-in formula

Excel has several formulae that can be accessed from the tool bar at the very top of the screen. In addition, you can calculate the formulae that are shown on a formula bar.

Filtering of the data and a variety of graphics in addition to that, it can filter data and display it using a variety of charts, including bar charts, pie charts, and so on.

Excel gives you several other options for how you may utilize the % formula, including the difference between two numbers, the total percentage, the percentage drop, the percentage rise, and many more of these options. You will go through all the relevant cases to have a deeper comprehension.

Let's begin by discussing how to open any Excel file on a computer if anybody here is unfamiliar with the process.

Percentage formula

Excel's tool bar has a % sign integrated into the program. It is often located in the middle of a toolbar, as illustrated in the following image:

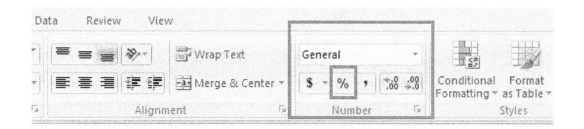

To turn a decimal number into a percentage, enter the decimal value into an Excel block, click on the block, and finally, click on the symbol for percentage (%) in the toolbar. The decimal figure that corresponds will have its equivalent percentage value translated for you.

Alternately, you may click the block that contains the decimal value and then hit the combination of Ctrl, Shift, & %. The decimal figure that corresponds will have its equivalent percentage value translated for you.

Examples depending on your percentage formula

Let's discuss several real-world applications of the % formula in Excel, covering various approaches.

Performing the calculations necessary to determine the percentages of 5 students across three disciplines.

The following is a breakdown of the performance of five students across three disciplines: Mathematics, English, and Science

Name	English	Mathematics	Science	Percentage
neha	76	79	82	
john	65	70	72	
Prince	62	75	69	
Swisha	82	90	88	
Tanu	54	62	72	

The following are the actions that need to be taken to compute the % of these three students:

The 1st thing you should to do is click on the first box in the % column, as seen in the following image:

Name	English	Mathematics	Science	Percentage
neha	76	79	82	
john	65	70	72	
Prince	62	75	69	
Swisha	82	90	88	
Tanu	54	62	72	

Step 2: Position your cursor within the formula bar, then click, hold, and write "= (click on column number D, click on column number E, click upon this column number F)/300."

The formula for it will be written as "= (C: C + D: D + E: E)/300%." The names of the columns are automatically supplied as C: C, D: D, and E: E in this instance.

The data value will be automatically converted into the % whenever the percentage sign is used. The formula shown above may alternatively be written as:

The equation for calculating a percentage is as follows: "== (C: C + D: D + E: E) / 300 * 100."

(Total points divided by number of topics multiplied by 100)

It will be shown on a formula bar in the following format:

f_x =(C:C+D:D+E:E)/300%

Name	English	Mathematics	Science	Percentage
neha	76	79	82	79
john	65	70	72	
Prince	62	75	69	
Swisha	82	90	88	
Tanu	54	62	72	

Press Enter. It will display the % value on the 1st block of a discount column.

After clicking once more on the 1st block in the % column, navigate your mouse to the block's lower-right corner and click there, as seen in the following image:

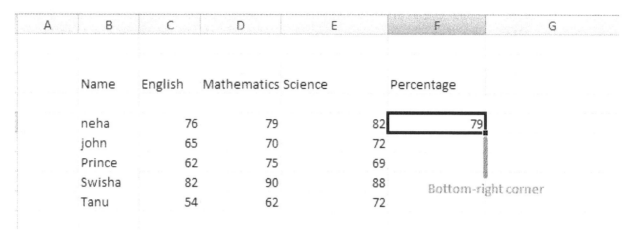

The next step is to move the point to a fifth box in the same column, which is labeled "Percentage," as illustrated in the following image:

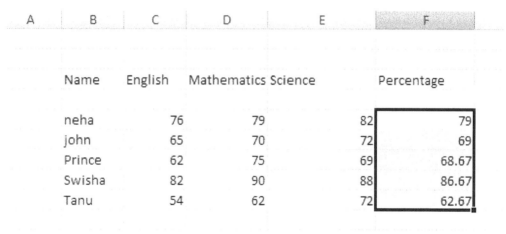

The computation of the % value will take place on its own. Similarly, you may quickly determine the proportion of many pupils in a class with only a single click.

Chapter 2: - Getting Started with Using Microsoft Excel

Microsoft Excel is software that allows you to create spreadsheets. People have to learn how to use Microsoft Excel as it helps them increase their productivity. Microsoft Excel is a simple-to-use program that is a crucial asset in any situation and critical for professional advancement.

From where to have Microsoft Excel?

Technology enthusiasts must appreciate Microsoft Office countless times for creating Microsoft Excel, which provides us with more headache relief than many other pain relievers. Microsoft's official website makes it simple to obtain this app. Use Google to find Microsoft's official website and click on the necessary links.

What is the right way to open Microsoft Excel?

To launch Microsoft Excel 2021, go over to the Start menu in Windows and pick Start All Programs. Then choose Microsoft Office, and finally, Microsoft Excel 2021. (If you don't have Excel, type it after clicking the start menu icon/selecting the tab.) A new, blank workbook has been launched, ready for you to fill in the details.

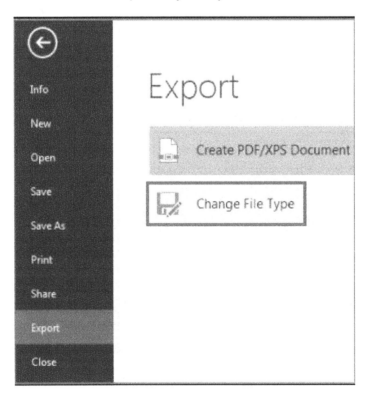

If you're attempting to open a file that has already been saved, you should first go through these steps.

Move 1: Open any XLSX file by double-clicking it.

To open XLSX files within Microsoft Excel, twice click the File. If you already have some version of MS Excel downloaded and installed on your computer (2016 or higher), double-clicking on a file will automatically open.

Move 2: Open Excel and drag - and - drop files within it.

If you already have Microsoft Excel installed on your computer, you can drag the XLSX file into an open spreadsheet in Microsoft Excel with a single mouse click. To do so, pick the XLSX file, keep down the left mouse button, drag the File further into an Excel spreadsheet that has already been opened, and then release the mouse button. It will then enable the XLSX sort file.

Move 3: Choose "Open with" from the right-click menu.

The pop-up menu will also allow you to open the File if you have some version of Microsoft Excel installed on your computer. Right-click the XLSX file with your mouse and select the "Open with" option. Following that, a window will appear that will suggest programs to open the File in question. The said File would open when you click on MS Excel. If MS Excel isn't mentioned, you haven't installed that on your computer.

Excel ribbon and its components

The MS Excel toolbar seems to be a row of tabs and icons above the MS Excel window that allows you to easily scan for, identify, and use commands to complete a task. It appears to be a complex toolbar, and it is. The toolbar was first introduced in Microsoft Excel 2007 to substitute the traditional toolbars and pull-down menus present in previous versions of MS Excel. Microsoft added the ability to configure the toolbar in MS Excel 2010.

Sections, command buttons, groups, and launcher dialogues are the four main components of the MS Excel 2021 toolbar.

The toolbar tab contains many groups of commands that are logically separated.

The toolbar group gathers identical commands and is used as part of a larger task.

A dialogue box launcher would be a small arrow in the group's lower right corner that keeps bringing up more commands that are similar. A dialogue box launcher appears in groups of commands that are larger than the available space.

A Command button would be the one that you press to complete a specific action.

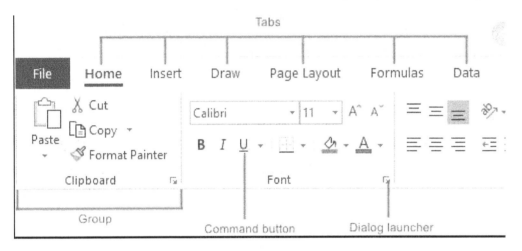

Standard Excel ribbon

File – Allows you to move to the backstage view, which contains the key file-related commands plus Microsoft Excel options. This tab was introduced in the MS Excel version of 2010 to substitute the Office button that was previously available in Microsoft Excel 2007 version. In previous versions, it was recognized as a File menu option.

Home – This section contains the most frequently used commands, such as copy/paste, sort and filter, formatting, and so on.

Insert – is being used to add images, formulas, diagrams, PivotTables, headers/footers, hyperlinks, and special signs to a worksheet.

Draw – This feature is dependent on the computer you're using; it enables you to draw anything you want, whether with a digital pen, a mouse or just with your finger.

Page Layout – Provides tools for customizing the template of Microsoft Excel worksheets, along with onscreen tabs. These tools monitor theme configurations, margins, grid lines, object orientation, page settings, and also print fields are all monitored by these tools.

Formulas – This section contains tools for incorporating features, naming them, and handling calculation options.

Data – Hold down the complete command to handle the data in a Microsoft Excel worksheet and link it to external data.

Review – It allows you to fix spelling errors, make tracking improvements, add feedback as well as notes, and save Microsoft Excel workbooks and worksheets.

View – Move between worksheet views, view, freeze panes and organize different windows.

Help – This tab provides quick access to the Help Task Pane of Excel, allowing one to notify Microsoft Support, request feedback, suggest new features, and quickly access training videos.

Developer's mode – gives one access to more advanced features such as Visual Standard Application macros, Microsoft Form controls plus Microsoft ActiveX, or even XML file commands. Since this tab is hidden, you must first toggle it before using it.

Add-ins – When you want to open some old workbook and sometimes activate an add-in that customizes the menu and a toolbar, this setting appears.

Tailor the work environment by understanding your worksheets

When you first start Microsoft Excel (by double-clicking its icon or choosing it off the Start menu), the software would ask you what you want to do. If you want to start a new spreadsheet, select the Blank Workbook option. A fresh workbook, including one blank sheet, will be created in Microsoft Excel.

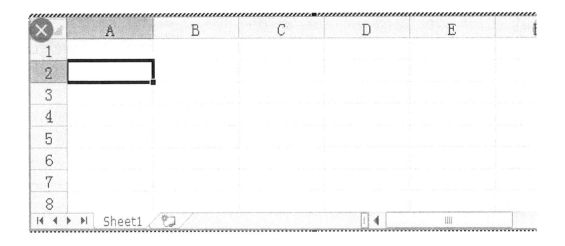

The horizontal axis has been interpreted as rows, whereas the vertical axis has been classified as columns; similarly, a selected box would be called a cell.

Customizing the Excel Workplace

The Microsoft Excel framework is designed to reflect things like using an excel application or how people use the MS Excel software. The components of Microsoft Excel are described below. The Microsoft Excel GUI aims to make MS Excel workbook operations as well as procedures more effective.

The Live Preview feature shows how the frame's formatting has improved. To see the format in the browser, drag the mouse cursor over the command.

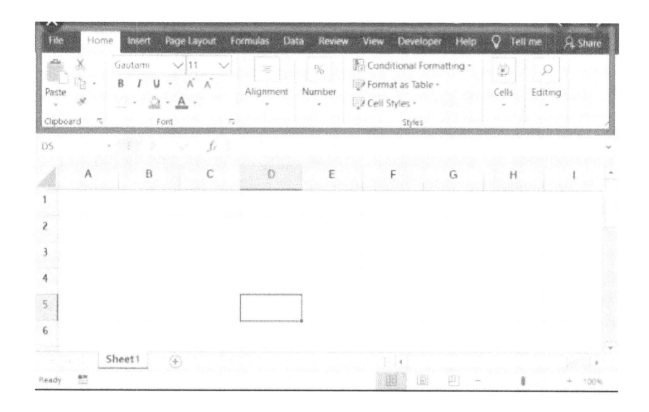

A few of the following configurations can be used by users to customize the working GUI.

Making a template in Excel

Open Microsoft Excel and create a new blank workbook.

The workbook must be saved with a specific file name in the specified folder.

Below are some additional tips and more detailed measures.

One must alter a few Excel workbook basics.

For example, font style and size: highlight the parts from each worksheet that you want to change, and then choose your options for number, alignment, and font style from its Font category just at the top of that same worksheet.

Column size/layout: Typically, you choose different column widths, select the columns or even the entire working sheet, and afterward change the width of the selected column.

In Print Settings, choose one or perhaps more worksheets, then go to Page Layout and then to Page Setting group to customize print settings, including header or footer, page orientation and page margins, and many other print layout settings.

Gridlines: Would you choose the gridlines on each worksheet to be darker? The dark borders or grid lines are visible but do not print. Select File> to go to Options > and then Advanced to adjust the gridline color. Then choose Display options for the existing worksheet and choose the title of its workbook from the drop-down menu. Finally, pick a specific gridline color under Display gridlines.

Worksheet count: one can insert and delete worksheets, as well as rename sheet tabs and adjust the color of worksheet tabs.

NOTE: When you introduce a new worksheet to your customized default workbook, the actual layout and formatting will be restored. You'll choose to attach extra worksheets to just the actual workbook to set aside an optional or main worksheet which you might copy if necessary.

Ribbon Customization

In Design, a Ribbon window is where you do the majority of your MS Excel Ribbon customizations. It's an option in Microsoft Excel. So, if you're going to start customizing the ribbon, you'll have to get one of the following:

Pick the Customize Ribbon option from the File tab > in the Options command

Right-click to customize the ribbon... from the context menu:

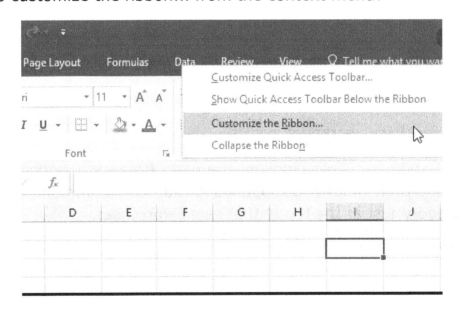

Introduce additional tabs in a ribbon

You can add your tab to that same Microsoft Excel ribbon to make your favorite commands easily available. Here's how to do it:

Choose the bottom list in tabs in the Customize Setting and Ribbon window, then press the New Tab Logo.

Since this would add a custom tab to a custom group, commands can only be used to add to one of the custom groups.

Select the Fresh Tab (Custom) tab you just created and click the Rename button to properly name it. Similarly, change the default name given by Microsoft Excel to a custom category with more detailed instructions. When it gets done, click OK to save the changes.

Deciding the theme's colors

Select Colors from the On-Page Layout Configuration tab within Microsoft Excel and pick a color you like.

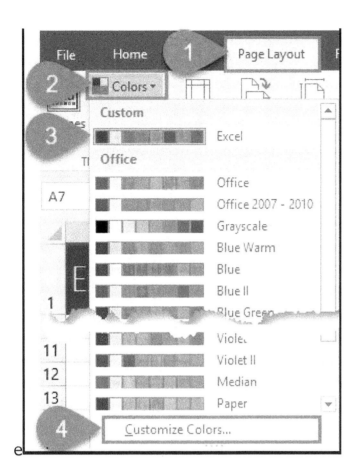

Working to develop your own color scheme

Choose Colors from the MS Excel Page Design configuration tab and also the Design setting feature, then Customize Colors.

Select a good color for the Colors' theme by pressing the button that is next to the theme color you want to change (for example, Accent 1 and Hyperlink).

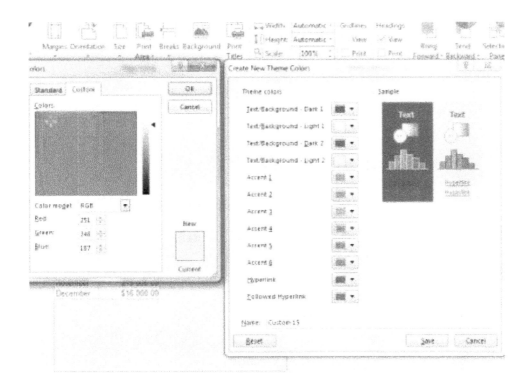

Go With more Colors, pick a good color from the Regular tab, and then insert code numbers of color, or have a color from its Customized tab to create your color theme.

A sample pane is where you can see a preview of the adjustments you've made.

You could repeat this procedure for the colors you want to alter.

In the name box, type the name you need for the new color scheme, then press the Save button.

Setting the formulas

First, go over towards the Formulas icon> Referred as Calculation group on a Microsoft Excel toolbar, press the Calculation Options button, and select the options below.

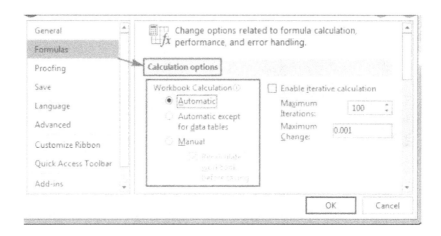

Automatic (default) - Instructs Microsoft Excel to recheck all conditional formulas for just any given formula, value, or name that is referenced for such formulas.

Automatic Excluding these Data Tables - Verify all related formulas automatically, except for those of the data tables.

Remember to distinguish between Microsoft Excel Tables (that is, Insert > Table) and Data Tables (Data > then What-If Study > and then Data Table), which also approximate numerous formula values. This choice disables automatic recalculation for data tables only, whereas regular Microsoft Excel tables are still calculated automatically.

Manual - disables Microsoft Excel's automatic calculation. Rechecking open workbooks is only possible if you're using any of these approaches.

Proofing options

Proof configurations change how Microsoft Excel corrects and then formats text as you write – this feature allows you to choose the configurations that are being used to automatically correct text as you type, as well as to save and reuse text or other items that you use frequently. Go to AutoCorrect Options, then choose the option that you want.

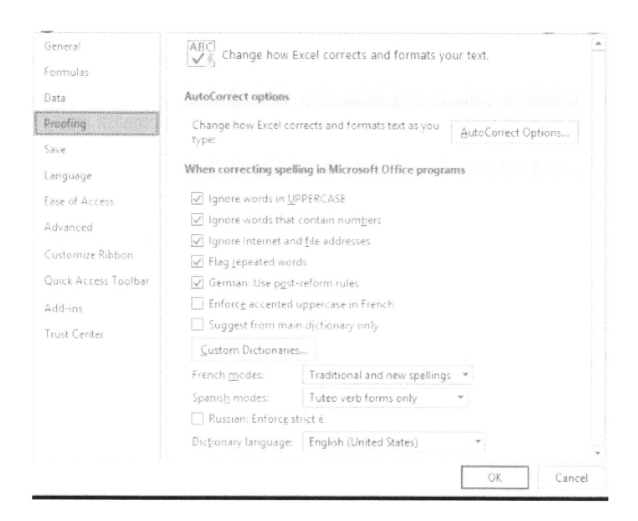

Words in UPPERCASE are ignored: In Microsoft Excel, words written in UPPERCASE characters should be ignored in a spelling search.

Ignoring words with numbers in a spelling search: Microsoft Excel-Ignore particular words with numbers during a spelling check.

Neglecting Internet and file addresses: If one wants Microsoft Word to automatically overlook Internet addresses, file names, as well as e-mail addresses, click this check box.

Flag repeated words: During every spelling search, this feature detects and marks words that are repeated.

Impose the accented uppercase: It displays magnified uppercase characters for French material.

Custom Dictionaries: Use this button to choose the vocabulary you want to use when testing spelling.

French modes: Sets spelling guidelines also for pronunciation of French words in the dictionary. In the above list box, pick the option you would like to keep.

Spanish modes: You must create spelling rules for Spanish words. Choose a separate option from the drop-down menu that will not appear in the list box.

Dictionary language: It enables users to choose which dictionary language they want to use.

The best tips for working with Excel

A collection of standard criteria for creating Microsoft Excel spreadsheets can be found here. They will help you work more efficiently and produce more structured data, so you must adhere to them.

Worksheet Development - By keeping all pertinent data in one tab, you could use Pivot Tables, functions, and Subtotals, including Worksheet Formulas.

Updated Performance - Compared to a smaller group of connected workbooks, fewer, bigger workbooks have improved overall performance.

Data Layout - Viewers normally search the rows and columns to get a sense of how the data is organized. Viewers can more effectively manage and evaluate data by first defining and presenting the most accurate information.

Protect the Cells - You can protect private cells and delicate ranges by limiting which users can edit or format them.

Data Validation Function - Any system that can assist in the removal of errors is definitely a time-saving feature that can keep the data up to date. This function can be found therein in the Data tab of the Data Tools category.

The Benefits of Using Color - Color is a great way to illustrate important details and give readers a break when reading a lot of information. It would be best if you used the various color options available in Conditional Formatting and Cell Types and the standard color options.

Absolute References - Do you need to keep the same cell's reference when copying or while using AutoFill? To avoid automatic content changes, use the "$" symbol.

Make a note for Simple calculations - When exchanging and creating formulas, mark the ranges and give the formulas a descriptive name. This will make it easier to select large amounts of data and comprehend the different formulas' intent.

Summary Sheets - Design the named range to just group the totals from every sheet you want to create a summary. If you'd like to summarize the total sheet, go to the feature menu and select the named range.

Using the Cell Merge Alternative - To make sorting easier, go to Format Cells, select Orientation, and then use Center By Range from the horizontal drop-down to center a label through several cells.

Chapter 3: - Understanding The Excel Interface

The Excel interface comprises fields, rows, columns, command bars, etc. The Excel screen will display when you open Excel. You can then create a workbook and choose any template.

There are so many different components of excel. It is essential to know all these elements of Microsoft excel to work on excel often. So, let's understand the entire interface of Microsoft Excel.

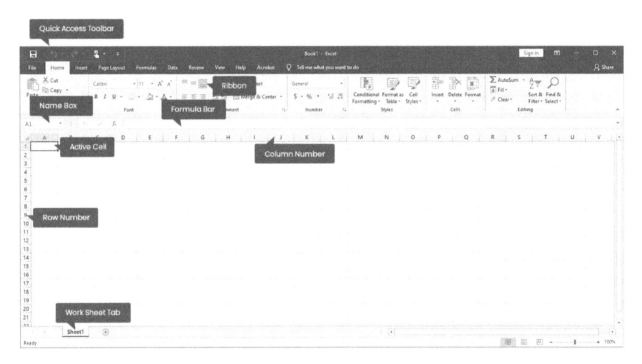

The two parts of Excel Interface:

- Front View

- Back View

How Excel Workbook Front View works

When we open Excel, we will see the excel display screen window. Below are various sources for understanding the spreadsheet and its elements.

- Recent Files
- Templates
- Back View
- Excel interface

- Excel Spreadsheet Back View

The element you should expect from this view:

➢ **Quick Access Toolbar** – This toolbar enables customization of frequently used commands to facilitate or expedite work. In addition, the quick access toolbar permits the user to map out any utility for expedited access.

➢ **Row Number** – This is a number attached to the address of different cells for the proper organization or work.

➢ **Sheet Tab** – This tab indicates the name of your sheets. By default, three sheets display in your new file. It gives the option to include additional new sheets to manage your work

➢ **Sheet Tab Button** – The sheet tab button helps users switch and scroll between invisible worksheets.

➢ **Status Bar** – The status bar displays various information about your active workbook by allowing you to view the application task's status. E.g. the Status of Scroll Lock, Numb Lock, Caps Lock, and different summary information regarding your data.

➢ **Horizontal Scroll Bar** – This bar allows you to enable your scroll sheet horizontally.

➢ **View Buttons** – This option give multiple consideration of sheets layout. E.g., Normal design, Page break preview, page layout.

➢ **Zoom Control** – This button enables you to view close, zoom in and zoom out. The zoom controls also allow the user to decrease or increase the levels of zoom enhancements of the worksheets.

➢ **Vertical Scroll bar** – This bar enables you to scroll down and up a sheet. It consists of vertical scroll bars that allow the user to quickly move the cursor through the worksheet in a vertical shape.

➢ **Ribbon Collapse Button** – The Ribbon Collapse button has a design that helps the user locate the necessary commands needed to complete specific tasks. These commands come in organized and logical groups placed together under several tabs. With this button, you can hide a ribbon from the top.

➢ **Close Button** – This button allows you to quit or exit MS Excel.

➢ **Maximize Button** – This button at the top of the screen allows you to maximize your Window.

➢ **Minimize Button** – This button is very close to the Maximize button, which is at the top of the screen, too. It helps you to minimize your Window.

➢ **Ribbon** – This is where all commands can be found and used. Once you click on the tab, it will change the controls displayed on the ribbon.

- ➤ **Formula Bar** – This bar in which a formula displays and helps in the active cell. The formula bars allow the user to edit or enter data while working on a worksheet.
- ➤ **Column Letters** – These letters show the address of different cells.
- ➤ **Active Cell** – This dark outline cell is an active cell you are currently working on.

These are the essential elements of Microsoft excel. Apart from all these, there are many other functions available in the excel application interface, which we will come to later.

Identification of the Screen Parts

The excel and worksheet window occupies the bulk of the screen. This grid gives a convenient workspace where you can manage your data. Surrounding the worksheet window are various command interfaces; each enables you to receive information about or apply functions to the data on the worksheet.

Title Bar

MS Excel's title bar is located in the quick access taskbar or at the Excel windows top corner and shows the name of a currently open file or document. The title bar additionally displays the name of the application and the open file. The title bar also displays the program name and the open file name.

Ribbon Tabs

To perform a common task in excel, you have to use the ribbon tab because it contains all you need. The Ribbon tab assists you in rapidly locating the instructions required to perform a job. The commands are split into different logical categories and grouped beneath each tab for easy access. Each tab represents a different work, such as writing or page layout. Some tabs are visible only when necessary to minimize clutter.

Spreadsheet

The spreadsheet helps to arrange, sort, and calculate data. It exists in rows and columns. Numeric values usually represent the data.

What Is A Cell?

A cell is the smallest and most potent element in an Excel spreadsheet. You can enter data into a cell by entering or copying and pasting. Text, numbers, and dates can all constitute data. Additionally, its borders, size, background color, and text color can be altered. These grids within Excel are referred to as cells. You can identify them by their column, reference, and row numbers, which appear at the cell's location.

What Is A Row?

A row is a discrete set of cells aligned horizontally from left to right. A single Excel spreadsheet contains 1048576 rows in total. Each row has a unique identification number ranging from 1 p to 1048576.

What Is A Column?

Columns are vertical arrays of cells aligned from the top to the bottom of the page. A single Excel worksheet contains 16384 columns, with each column identified by a letter range from A to XFD. By clicking on the column header, a user can select a certain column.

Chapter 4: - MS Excel graphs and charts

What Are Excel Graphs & Charts?

Graphs and charts help you make sense of the data by visualizing quantitative numbers in a simple option. Despite the fact that the names are sometimes used indiscriminately, they are distinct. Graphs are indeed the simplest basic visual representation of data, and they often show data point values across time. Charts are more complicated because they enable you to contrast parts of a set of data to certain other data in the same set. Charts are also much more visually appealing than graphs because they frequently have a more distinctive shape than just a standard x- & y-axis.

In presentations, graphs and charts are frequently used to provide a fast overview of progress or outcomes to management, clients, or team members. You can make a graph or chart to depict almost any type of quantitative data, saving you the effort and time of sifting through spreadsheets to uncover links & trends.

Excel makes it simple to construct graphs and charts, particularly because you can save the data in your Excel Workbook instead of transferring it from another tool. Excel also comes with a number of pre-made chart & graph kinds from which you can choose the one which best illustrates the information relationship(s) you wish to emphasize.

Excel has a huge chart or graph library to help you graphically present the data. While numerous chart types may "work" for a particular data set, it's critical to choose one that best suits the narrative you want to tell with the data. You may, of course, add graphical components to a graph or chart to enhance & customize it. There seem to be five main types of graphs and charts in Excel 2016.

Column Charts: Column charts are one of the most often used charts and are best utilized to compare data or if you get numerous divisions of one parameter. Choose the visualization that best tells the story of your data.

Bar Charts: The fundamental difference between a bar chart as well as a column chart is that the bars inside a bar chart are horizontal rather than vertical. While bar charts and column charts can frequently be used equally, some people prefer column charts when dealing using negative values since it's easier to visualize negatives vertically on the y-axis.

Pie Charts: Utilize pie charts when analyzing percentages of the whole ("whole" refers to the sum of the data's values). Every value is expressed by a pie slice, allowing you to see the proportions. There are five varieties of pie charts: pie, pie of pie (which divides one pie into two to display sub-category ratios), 3-D pie, the bar of pie & doughnut.

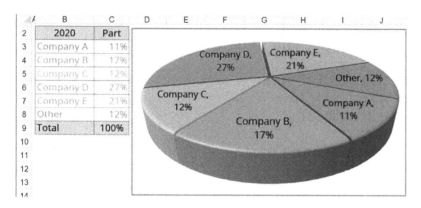

Line Charts: Instead of static pieces of data, a line chart is best for depicting trends and patterns. The lines are connected by each data point, allowing you to observe how well the value(s) grew or dropped over time. Line, stacked line, hundred percent stacked line, line having markers, stacked line having markers, 100 percent stacked line with indicators, & 3-D line are the 7 line chart possibilities.

Scatter Charts: Scatter charts are being used to illustrate how each variable influences another. They are comparable to line graphs in that they are helpful for demonstrating variation in variables over time. (This is referred to as correlation.) Bubble charts, which are a common chart form, are classified as scatter.

In addition, there are 4 minor categories. These graphs are more case-specific in nature:

Area: Area charts, like line charts, depict variations in numbers over time. Region charts, on the other hand, are good for highlighting differences in variation among numerous variables since the area below each line is solid.

Stock: This sort of chart is often used in financial research & by investors to represent the low, high, & closing price of a stock Surface charts, on the other hand, might be hard to read, so be sure the audience is comfortable with them. 3-D surface, contour, wireframe contour, and wireframe 3-D are all options.

Radar: A radar chart is useful for displaying data from numerous variables with respect to one another. The central point is the starting point for all variables. The key to using radar charts seems to be to compare all individual factors in relation to one another; they're frequently used to compare the strengths & weaknesses of various products or personnel. Radar, radar with markings, and filled radar are the three forms of radar charts.

Using Insert Chart To Make Charts

Follow the instructions below; to generate charts, you must use the Insert Chart tab.

Step 1: Choose the information you want to use.

Step 2: On the Ribbon, select the Insert tab.

Step 3: On the Ribbon, select Insert Column Chart.

The options for 2-D column and 3-D column charts are shown. A More Column Charts... option is also available.

Step 4: View the previews by moving through into the Column Chart settings.

Step 5: Select Clustered Column from the drop-down menu. The graph will appear on the worksheet.

Step 6: Edit Chart Title to give the chart a suitable title.

Using Recommended Charts To Make Charts

You may use the Recommended Charts feature if:

- If you want to generate a chart quickly
- You're unsure which chart type will best suit your data.
- If, indeed, the chart style you choose doesn't work with the data, try a different one.

Follow the instructions below in using the Recommended Charts option:

Step 1: Choose the information you want to use.

Step 2: On the Ribbon, select the Insert tab.

Step 3: Select Recommended Charts from the drop-down menu.

Underneath the tab of Recommended Charts, a popup presents the charts which best suit the data will appear.

Step 4: Look at the Charts We Recommend.

Step 5: Upon that right side, select the chart type to obtain a preview.

Step 6: Pick a chart type that appeals to you. Click the OK button. The graph will appear on your worksheet.

If you don't find a chart that you like, go and select the All Charts page to look at all the chart types offered and choose one.

Step 7: Modify Chart Title to provide the chart with a suitable title.

Using Quick Analysis To Create Charts

To make a chart using Quick Analysis, follow the steps below:

Step 1: Choose the information you want to use.

A button for a quick analysis The Quick Analysis button displays just at the bottom right of the data you've chosen.

Step 2: Select the Quick Analysis icon from the toolbar.

The CHARTS, TABLES, FORMATTING, and SPARKLINES options appear in the Quick Analysis toolbar.

Step 3: Select CHARTS from the drop-down menu.

Charts that are recommended for the data will then be displayed.

Step 4: Hover on the Recommended Charts with your mouse. There will be samples of the accessible charts.

Step 5: Select "More."

There will be a lot more Recommended Charts presented.

Step 6: Select the chart type you want, then click OK. A chart will appear on the worksheet.

Step 7: Edit Chart Title to give the chart a suitable title.

Types Of Excel Charts

Excel has a variety of charts to choose from, depending on your needs. You can make a chart depending on the specific type of data you have. You may modify the chart type at any time.

The major chart kinds available in Excel are:

- Line Chart

- Pie Chart

- Column Chart

- Bar Chart

- Doughnut Chart

- XY (Scatter) Chart

- Stock Chart

- Radar Chart

- Area Chart

- Bubble Chart

- Surface Chart

There are sub-categories for each one of these chart kinds. This section will provide you with a description of the different chart kinds as well as the sub-types which each chart type has.

Column Chart

In a Column Chart, the horizontal (classification) axis is used to show the categories, while the vertical (valuation) axis is used to display the values. Organize your data in rows or columns on the worksheet to make a column chart.

The sub-types of a column chart are as follows:

Stacked Column

Clustered Column

100% Stacked Column

3-D Clustered Column

Stacked Column

3-D Column

3-D 100% Stacked Column.

Line Chart

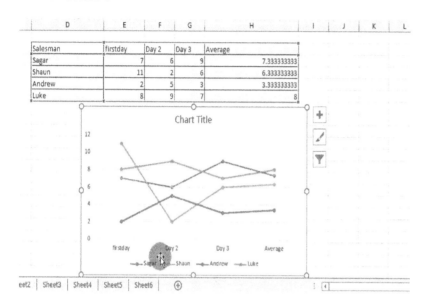

On an equally scaled Axis, line charts may represent continuous data across time. As a result, they're great for displaying data patterns at regular periods, such as quarters, months, or years.

In a line graph, you can see:

The horizontal axis is uniformly distributed with category data.

The vertical axis is uniformly dispersed with valuable data.

Organize your data in rows or columns on the spreadsheet to make a line chart.

The following are the sub-types of a line chart:

3-D line

Line

Hundred percent Stacked Line

Stacked Line

Stacked Line with Markers

Line with Markers

100% Stacked Line having Markers

Pie Chart

The size of elements in a single data series is proportional to the total of the elements in a pie chart. In a pie chart, all data points are represented as a proportion of the total pie. Organize the data in a single row or column on the spreadsheet to make a Pie Chart.

The following are the sub-types of a pie chart:

Bar of Pie

3-D pie

Pie

Pie of Pie

Doughnut Chart

The link between parts and the whole is depicted in a doughnut chart. A Doughnut Chart is identical to a Pie Chart, with the exception that a Doughnut Chart may include multiple data series while a Pie Chart may only have one.

A Doughnut Chart is made up of rings, all representing a different data series. Organize the data in rows or columns on your worksheet to make a Doughnut Chart.

Bar Chart

Individual item comparisons are depicted using bar charts. In Bar Charts, the classifications are organized all along the vertical axis as well as the values are structured all along the horizontal axis. Organize your data in rows or columns on the worksheet to make a Bar Chart.

The following are the sub-types of a bar chart:

3-D 100% Stacked bar

Clustered Bar

100% Stacked Bar

Stacked Bar

3-D Stacked Bar

3-D Clustered Bar

Area Chart

Area charts are best for plotting change with time and highlighting the combined value along with a trend. The area chart describes the correlation of components to a whole by displaying the total of the plotted data. Organize your data in rows or columns on the spreadsheet to make an Area Chart.

The following are the sub-types of an Area Chart:

Stacked Area

Area

3-D Area

100% Stacked Area

3-D 100% Stacked Area

3-D Stacked Area

XY (Scatter) Chart

XY (Scatter) charts are typically commonly used to display and compare quantitative quantities, such as data from science, statistics, and engineering.

There are two Value Axes in a Scatter chart:

Axis of Value Horizontal (x)

Axis of Vertical Value (y)

It merges x & y information into a single number & shows them in clusters of irregular intervals. Organize your data in rows and columns on the spreadsheet to make a Scatter chart.

Put all x values in a single row or column, then the value of y in the subsequent rows or columns.

When utilizing a scatter chart, keep the following in mind:

You would like to adjust the horizontal axis scale.

You should use a logarithmic scale for that axis.

The horizontal axis values really aren't equally distributed.

On the horizontal axis, there are a whole lot of data points.

To display more statistics that comprise pairs or clustered groups of values, you wish to modify your independent axis levels of a scatter chart.

Instead of showing disparities between data points, you would like to illustrate commonalities between big amounts of data.

You wish to compare a large number of data points over a long period of time.

Therefore more data you put in your scatter chart, the more accurate your comparisons will be.

The following are the sub-types of a scatter chart:

Scatter

Smooth Lines & Markers are being used to scatter.

Smooth Lines to Scatter

Scatter having Markers & Straight Lines

Using Straight Lines to Scatter

Bubble Chart

A Bubble chart looks similar to a Scatter chart; only it has a 3rd column that specifies the thickness of the bubbles that reflect all data points inside the data series.

The following are the several types of bubble charts:

Bubble

Three-dimensional bubble

Stock Charts

Stock charts, as the title suggests, can depict price movements in stocks. A Stock chart, on the other hand, will be used to display changes in those other data, including average precipitation or yearly temperatures.

Organize your data in rows or columns in a specified arrangement on your worksheet to make a stock chart. To make a simple rising Stock chart, for example, organize the data with Low, Close, and High as Column names in that sequence.

The following are the sub-types of a stock chart:

Open-High-Low-Close

High-Low-Close

Volume-Open-High-Low-Close

Volume-High-Low-Close

Surface Chart

When you need to determine the best combinations of 2 variables, a Surface chart comes in handy. Colors & patterns, just like on a topographic map, identify areas with similar values.

To make a Surface chart, follow these steps:

Make that the categories & data series would both be numeric values.

Organize the data on your worksheet in rows or columns.

The following are the sub-types of a surface chart:

Wireframe 3-D Surface

3-D surface

Wireframe Contour

Contour

Radar Chart

The cumulative values of many data series are compared using radar plots. Organize the data in rows or columns on your worksheet to make a Radar chart.

The following are the sub-types of a radar chart:

Radar

Markers and Radar

Radar that has been filled

Combo Chart

Combo charts merge 2 or more than 2 chart types in order to make data easier to comprehend, particularly whenever the data is complex. It has an additional axis that makes it more easier to understand. Organize your data in rows and columns on the spreadsheet to make a Combo chart.

The following are the sub-types of a Combo chart:

Line – Clustered Column

Clustered Column – Secondary Axis Line

Clustered Column – Stacked Area

Custom Combination

Creating several charts type

Chapter 5: - Tables & Their Importance

A table is a useful method for managing and arranging data together in Excel. Define a table to be a distinct group of multiple rows and columns in a spreadsheet, contrasted to a list. You may have numerous tables on the same page if you want to be more organized.

Your data in a Spreadsheet may be already organized into a table since it's organized into rows and columns and is all in one place. However, unless you've utilized the special Excel data table function, your data isn't organized in a real "table" format.

To make it simpler to manage and analyze a set of linked data, you may create an Excel table from a variety of cells in your spreadsheet. Tables may be the most useful tool in Excel that you're not currently making use of. In Excel, creating a table is a simple process. A data table may be created from flat data in only a few clicks (or by using a single keyboard shortcut). This has a number of advantages over a flat data table.

There are several benefits to using an Excel table, including the following:

1.   Styles in a hurry. Add color, banded rows, or header styles with a single click to your data to make it more visually appealing.

2.   Table headings. Give tables a name so they can be referred to in other calculations more easily.

3.   Formulas that are less polluting. When working in a table, Excel formulas are considerably simpler to understand and write than when working in a spreadsheet.

4.   The auto-expand feature is enabled. In Excel, when you add a new row and column to your information, the table is instantly updated to accommodate the newly added cells.

5.   Filters and subtotals are included. As you filter your data, automatic filter icons and subtotals have added that change as you do.

Table Types

In Excel, we can build three different sorts of tables. These are the ones:

A general Excel table, sometimes known as an "Excel Table"

If the rows or columns of the data are specified, a standard Excel table is a critical component for grouping the information. A single Excel worksheet page may include many tables, each of which can be referenced in formulae by their respective header titles. Data in Excel appears to be in a tabular form since information is collected in the grid format in the spreadsheet. However, by definition, it is not regarded as a table in Microsoft Excel. It is necessary to define a range of collections of cells as a table before they may be used.

Informational Table

The Data table is a very intriguing tool discovered in the What-If Research feature of Microsoft Excel, and is extremely easy to use. With the help of a data table, we may compute any argument that depends on a variety of factors. The formula is applied to a data table, and the value changes as a result of one or two aspects in the table being changed.

The PivotTable is the third item on the list.

The PivotTable is a particular Excel table tool that allows you to rearrange the columns and rows of a data collection in any way you like. In fact, this tool makes no modifications to the original data; instead, it changes the data direction and generates some unique outputs from the data. When dealing with a huge quantity of data, the PivotTable comes in handy. It saves us time by allowing us to calculate quickly. It can also execute various operations, such as sum, mean, sort, grouping, and count, among others.

How Can You Make a Table in Excel?

We'll go through the process of creating several types of Excel tables in this section. In this part, we'll go over how to make a generic Excel table, as well as its specific features, and its advantages and disadvantages, all with a full explanation.

How to Build an Excel Table in Microsoft Excel

To construct an Excel Table, follow the instructions outlined in this section:

1. To begin, choose any column or row in the database by clicking on it.

2. Then, choose the home option from the drop-down menu.

3. Then, using the Styles tool, pick the Style as a Table option.

4. Choose any of the predefined table styles.

5. Alternatively, we might use the keyboard shortcut Ctrl+T.

6. Create Table will be the name of the new dialogue box displayed.

7. If the data set has any headers, choose the My table includes headers checkbox.

8. Now, click on the OK button.

Pivot Table

What Is Pivot Table?

A pivot table is primarily a tool for creating data summaries from data sources. By just clicking & dragging information from one region of report to another, you may quickly summarize data. It can turn thousands of columns and rows of data into information that is useful. On every level of data, you may choose to show subtotals. Interactivity of these tables is maybe their greatest benefit. Information may be changed without any effort. Fact that you may "pivot" data in any direction makes it clear why they are named pivot tables.

Why Pivot Tables Are Used?

Why then should you use a pivot table? If you wish to condense a lot of data, such a table should be employed. It will take more time to attempt to summarize data using Excel formulae because you must manually create calculations. You may need to change your calculations if you add new information to data, which might take time. While manually constructed tables with formulae might take longer to prepare, pivot tables can be simply formatted to render them presentable and aesthetically pleasing. Using formulae to summarize your data in a very big data collection with thousands of columns and rows can prolong computation time in Excel. Algorithms will take some time to recalculate every time you modify your data. You won't have any issues with sluggish computation times while using pivot tables.

Table Layout

Pivot table pane houses pivot table's four components. Connected with pivot tables, Pivot Fields is function pane that by default sits on window's right side. pivot table's 4 elements are:

1) Filters
2) Rows
3) Columns
4) Values

In below screenshot, there are 5 fields (Area, Product, Month, Sales, Units). These are column headings in source data. pivot table appearance & information will be shown by what fields you add in 4 areas of table Fields. Now I will explain each area in turn.

Filters

With the use of filters, you can only view the data you would like to see while hiding the rest. You may then choose which field's items you wish to view or not by marking or disabling boxes after moving a field to the Filters section. They function similarly to a table filter. The area field in the example below is filtered.

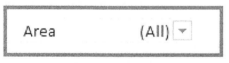

Sum of Sales	Jan	Feb	Mar	Apr	May	Grand Total
Mouse			500			500
Mouse mat				134		134
PC		5600				5600
Printer	250					250
Scanner					540	540
Grand Total	250	5600	500	134	540	7024

Rows

Each field item is shown in a distinct row in rows. One row makes up one field item. They approach the table's left side from below. In the example below, the Product area is in the Rows section, and each row displays items from the Product field.

Area   (All) ▼

Sum of Sales						
	Jan	Feb	Mar	Apr	May	Grand Total
Mouse			500			500
Mouse mat				134		134
PC		5600				5600
Printer	250					250
Scanner					540	540
Grand Total	250	5600	500	134	540	7024

Columns

Every field item is shown across many columns in columns. The Month field is in the Columns section in the sample below, & every item in the Month field is in a different column.

Area   (All) ▼

Sum of Sales						
	Jan	Feb	Mar	Apr	May	Grand Total
Mouse			500			500
Mouse mat				134		134
PC		5600				5600
Printer	250					250
Scanner					540	540
Grand Total	250	5600	500	134	540	7024

Values

Values provide a summary of data. Sales field is in the Values section in the sample below. The pivot table below provides a month-by-month breakdown of sales by product. Excel provides a variety of summary options, including COUNT, SUM, AVERAGE, MIN, MAX, and more. At least one field must be filled out in the Values box. The same field may appear twice in the Values box. For instance, you might use a pivot table to display the total sales as well as the average sales by product and month.

Area   (All) ▼

Sum of Sales						
	Jan	Feb	Mar	Apr	May	Grand Total
Mouse			500			500
Mouse mat				134		134
PC		5600				5600
Printer	250					250
Scanner					540	540
Grand Total	250	5600	500	134	540	7024

Displaying Pivot table Fields Pane

Whenever you click on Pivot table, Pivot table Field pane will automatically appear. If for any reason it doesn't appear, then click any cell in Pivot table, and from ribbon, click on **Analyze** tab. Under **Show,** group click on **Field List** command button.

Structure of Data Source

In order to create Pivot table, you need to ensure that your data source is structured correctly. This means your data must be rectangular in shape and stored in a worksheet range or a table. In order to change your worksheet range to a table, select a cell anywhere in data and then from ribbon, click **Insert** tab and, under **Tables** group, select **Table** command button.

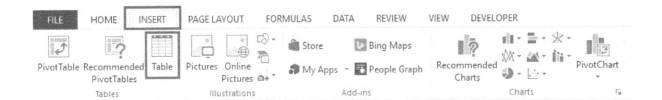

Data to create Pivot tables needs to contain two types of fields:

1) **Data** – This is usually a value to be summarized. For example, Sales field is data field

2) **Category** – This describes data. For example, Product, Area, and Month fields are category fields

It is also important to note that your data source must contain headings on all columns; otherwise, you will get below message.

Updating Pivot Tables

Whenever you update data source, Pivot table will not update immediately like with formulas. This is one of downsides of using pivot tables instead of formulas. When you create Pivot table, Excel stores that data in a Pivot Cache. Pivot Cache is automatically generated whenever you create Pivot table. It is like a container that stores data source. Whenever you make changes to Pivot table, it doesn't use data source but Pivot Cache instead.

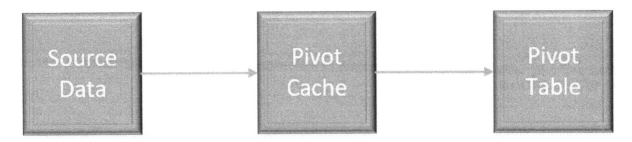

So why is there a Pivot Cache? Well, Pivot Cache is there to optimize functionality of Pivot table. It helps Pivot table summarise information instantly whenever you drag and drop fields in Filters, Rows, Columns, and Values areas in Pivot table Fields pane.

This is reason why Pivot table will not update straight away when you change source data. In order to update Pivot table when source data has changed, you must refresh Pivot table.

How to Create a Basic Pivot Table?

In this chapter, I will show you step-by-step instructions on how to create Pivot table.

Specifying Source Data

First thing you need to do is to specify what data you want to use to create Pivot table. To do this, follow these instructions:

1) Select any cell in data range. Click on **INSERT** tab in ribbon, and then under **Tables** group, select **PivotTable** command button

2) Create PivotTable dialog box will appear. Excel will attempt to specify correct range of data based on active cell. If for any reason, Excel doesn't specify correct range, then you can use your mouse to select data range. In this example, I selected range

A1:F22. Data range will appear in **Table/Range** field

Specifying Location of Pivot table

Next step is to specify where you want Pivot table to be located. You can specify whether to have Pivot table in a new worksheet or in existing worksheet from Create PivotTable dialog box. In this example, I have selected **New Worksheet**. Choose Existing Worksheet & then provide a cell's location in Location form if you need a pivot table in an existing worksheet. After doing this, press the OK button.

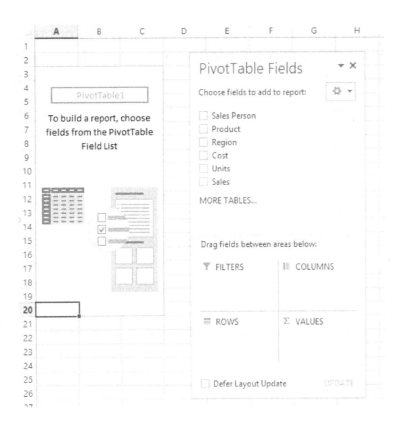

Adding Fields to Pivot table

You now need to build Pivot table by moving fields in Filters, Columns, Rows, & Values area of Fields pane. In this example, I want to show sales by product and sales person. You can move fields into one of four areas of Pivot table pane by using one of following methods:

1) Clicking and dragging fields to one of four areas.

2) Right-click field name and choose one of four areas in shortcut menu. You can select from Add to Labels in Row, Add to Labels in Column, Add to Filter Report or to Values. You can also add a field as a slicer.

3) Select check box against appropriate field. Excel will do its best to move it to correct area. Like, when I saw field of Sales Person, it rightly moved it to Rows area. When you check box for field that has values, Excel will then move it to Values area. If Excel shifts field to area you do not want it to be in, then you can simply do one of first two options to move it to correct area.

In the example, I have made Pivot table that illustrates what items are sold by each Sales person with amount for each item. There is also a subtotal which shows total sales sold by each Sales person.

Sales person and Product fields are in Rows area, and Sales is in Values area of Pivot table Fields pane.

Reorganizing Pivot table

Once you have created Pivot table, it is very easy to change it around to show different information. By pivoting fields, you can answer different questions and look at different trends and patterns. To move fields in another area in Fields pane, click & drag field to some other area or right-click field and select one of options in menu as described in previous section. In this section, I will show you how easy it is to modify the pivot tables to make another summary information.

Show Sales for East Area Only

In below example, I want to see all sales for East area only. For this, I put Region field in Filters area of Pivot table Fields pane. Filter will now display above Pivot table. I then just checked East check box and unselected other check boxes, and then pressed OK button.

Pivot table now just displays information relating to East area only.

Show Total Sales by Furniture Item

In this example, I just want to see total sales for each furniture item. I removed Sales Person field by clicking it and dragging it away. Pivot table now displays total sales for each furniture item. You can make this more meaningful by sorting sales in descending order so you can easily see which furniture has made most sales through to which has made least sales.

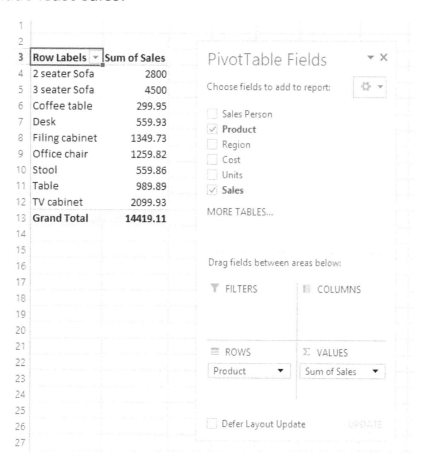

Show Sales by Area

In this example, I want to see what furniture items were sold in each area and see total sales by area. I have put Region field in Columns area of Pivot table Fields pane, so each area is a column heading. Product field is in area of Rows, so furniture items occupy a row. Sales is Values area of Fields pane.

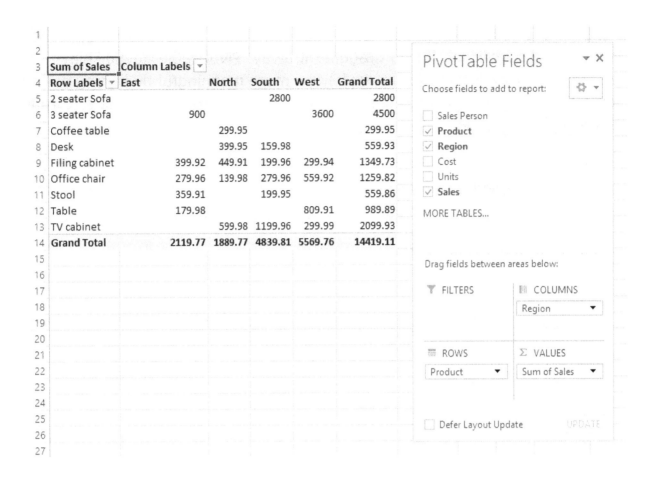

Sum of Sales	Column Labels				
Row Labels	East	North	South	West	Grand Total
2 seater Sofa			2800		2800
3 seater Sofa	900			3600	4500
Coffee table		299.95			299.95
Desk		399.95	159.98		559.93
Filing cabinet	399.92	449.91	199.96	299.94	1349.73
Office chair	279.96	139.98	279.96	559.92	1259.82
Stool	359.91		199.95		559.86
Table	179.98			809.91	989.89
TV cabinet		599.98	1199.96	299.99	2099.93
Grand Total	2119.77	1889.77	4839.81	5569.76	14419.11

Show Total Sales Made by Sales Person

In this example, I want to see which Sales person has made most sales. Sales person is in Rows area, and Sales is in Values area of Pivot table Fields pane. Again, to make this more meaningful, you would normally sort this in descending order of sales, so you get to see who top Sales person is through to Sales person who has made least sales.

Refreshing Pivot table

As mentioned in previous chapter, if source data is updated, Pivot table will not automatically update. You need to update Pivot table by refreshing it to reflect new changes. There are two ways to do this:

Method 1

From ribbon, click **Data** tab, and under **Connections** group, click on **Refresh All** command button.

Method 2

Right-click any cell in Pivot table, and in shortcut menu, select **Refresh**.

Changes to Data Source

If your data source has changed and you have inserted new columns at end, then Pivot table will not use these new columns unless you re-define range.

	Sales Person	Product	Region	Cost	Units	Sales	Sales Date	Month	Year
1	Sales Pers	Product	Regio	Cost	Units	Sales	Sales Date	Month	Year
2	Jim	Desk	North	$79.99	5	$399.95	04/08/2019	Aug	2019
3	Sally	Office chair	South	$69.99	4	$279.96	05/08/2019	Aug	2019
4	Jim	Office chair	North	$69.99	2	$139.98	07/11/2019	Nov	2019
5	John	Filing cabinet	East	$49.99	8	$399.92	19/11/2019	Nov	2019
6	Lisa	Table	West	$89.99	9	$809.91	22/11/2019	Nov	2019
7	Sally	Filing cabinet	South	$49.99	4	$199.96	04/12/2019	Dec	2019
8	Lisa	3 seater Sofa	West	$900.00	4	$3,600.00	08/12/2019	Dec	2019
9	Jim	Filing cabinet	North	$49.99	9	$449.91	15/12/2019	Dec	2019
10	John	Table	East	$89.99	2	$179.98	21/12/2019	Dec	2019
11	Sally	2 seater Sofa	South	$700.00	4	$2,800.00	04/01/2020	Jan	2020
12	Lisa	Office chair	West	$69.99	8	$559.92	09/01/2020	Jan	2020
13	John	Stool	East	$39.99	9	$359.91	19/01/2020	Jan	2020
14	Jim	Coffee table	North	$59.99	5	$299.95	04/02/2020	Feb	2020
15	Sally	TV cabinet	South	$299.99	4	$1,199.96	08/02/2020	Feb	2020
16	Lisa	Filing cabinet	West	$49.99	6	$299.94	19/02/2020	Feb	2020
17	John	3 seater Sofa	East	$900.00	1	$900.00	06/03/2020	Mar	2020
18	Jim	TV cabinet	North	$299.99	2	$599.98	07/03/2020	Mar	2020
19	Sally	Stool	South	$39.99	5	$199.95	17/03/2020	Mar	2020
20	Lisa	TV cabinet	West	$299.99	1	$299.99	02/04/2020	Apr	2020
21	John	Office chair	East	$69.99	4	$279.96	28/04/2020	Apr	2020
22	Sally	Desk	South	$79.99	2	$159.98	07/05/2020	May	2020

To do this, follow these steps:

1) Click on Pivot table

2) In ribbon, click on **Analyse** tab, and under **Data** group, click **Change Data Source** command button

73

3) Excel will take you back to data source, and Change PivotTable Data Source dialog box will appear

4) You then select range again, including new columns in the

Table/Range field and then press **OK** button

5) Refresh Pivot table as described in previous section

6) three new fields are now included in Pivot table Fields pane

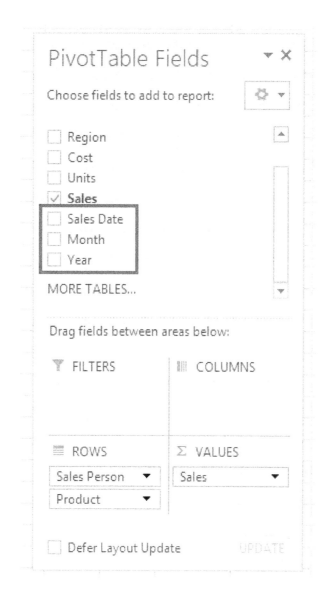

Changing Calculation in Pivot table

By default, Excel will summarize data in Pivot table by summing values. You can change calculation to show count, average, maximum value, minimum value, and so on. Here are steps to change calculation from Sum to Average:

1) Click any cell in Pivot table

2) Click on field in Values area of Pivot table Fields pane where you want to change calculation. In this example, I click on Sales field. From menu select

Value Field Settings

3) In Value Field Settings dialog box, select desired calculation under **Summarize value field**. In this example, I select **Average**. Once you have selected calculation, click **OK** button

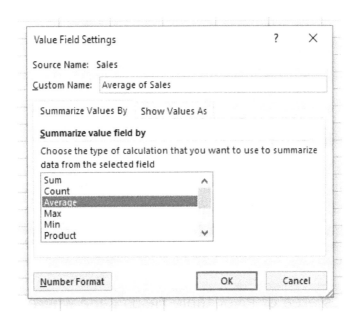

Customizing Pivot table

Now that I have taken you through steps of how to create Pivot table, I will now show you how to customize Pivot table so it looks more professional, visually appealing, and easier to understand and interpret. There are various ways to customize and format pivot tables, and this chapter will explain how you can achieve this. I will use same pivot table I created in previous chapter.

Changing Pivot Table Styles

Whenever you create Pivot table, Excel applies default pivot table style. This looks dull and not very attractive to look at, especially if you are sending it to your manager or customer. Excel has many pivot tables styles which you can apply, so your pivot table stands out and looks more pleasing to eye.

Here are steps to apply Pivot table style:

1) Click a cell in Pivot table

2) Click **Design** tab from ribbon. In **PivotTable Styles** group, click on down arrow at bottom right to see all available styles you can choose from.

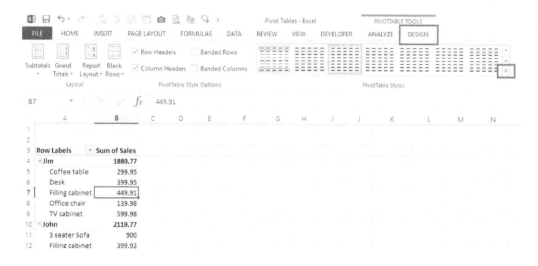

3) If you hover your mouse over different pivot table styles, you can see style being applied to Pivot table. Once you are happy with a style, just click your left mouse button to apply it to Pivot table. In this example, I have selected 'Pivot Style Medium 2'.

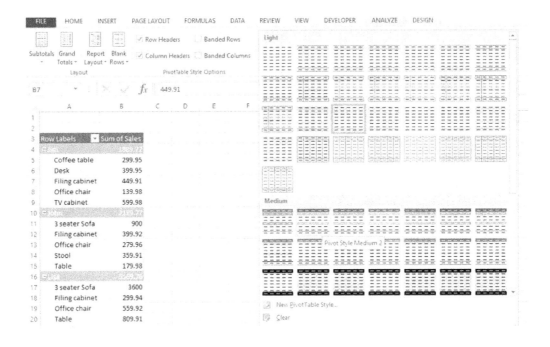

Create a New Pivot Table Style

If you don't like any of Pivot table styles Excel has to offer, then you can create your own. For this example, I want to create Pivot table style that colors Pivot table grey and has a border around it. Here are steps on how you can do this:

1) Select a cell in Pivot table

2) From ribbon, click **Design** tab. In **PivotTable Styles,** group click on down arrow, which is located on bottom right

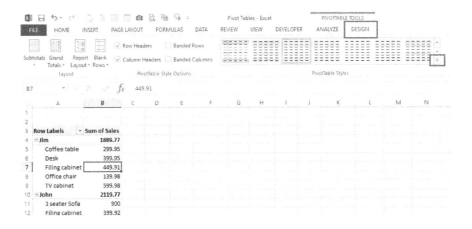

3) Select New PivotTable Style

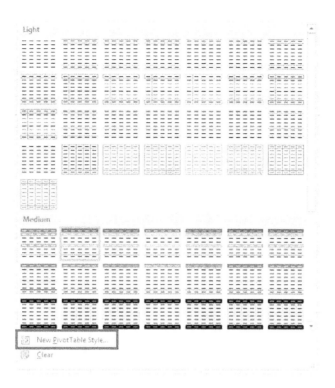

4) New dialog style box for pivot table will appear. You can name your new custom pivot table style in **Name** field. I have called this style 'Example.'

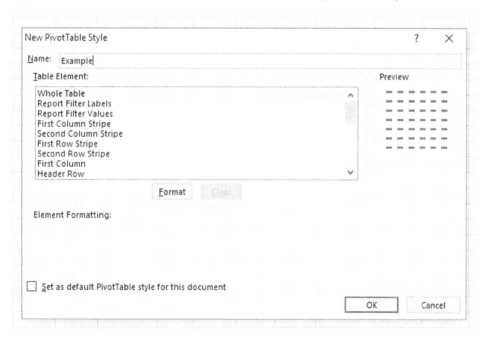

5) I want to make whole pivot table grey and apply a border around it, so I select **Whole Table** under **Table Element** and then select **Format** button.

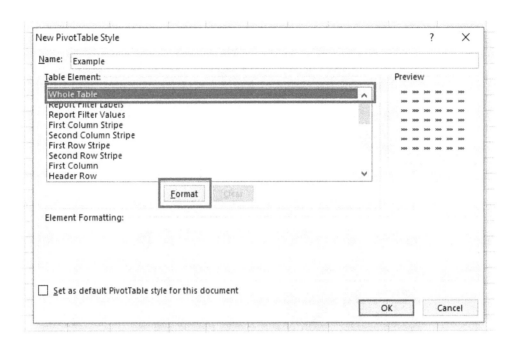

6) In **Fill** tab, I select a grey color

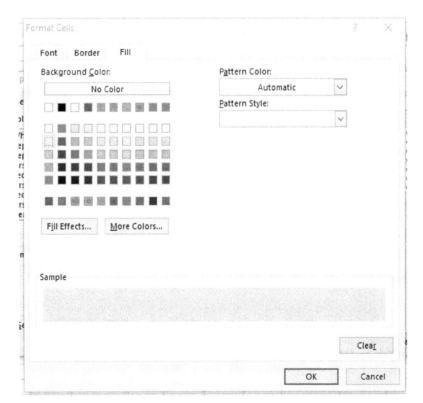

7) I then click on **Border** tab and select a line style under **Line Style** section and apply it in **Border** section to all edges. I then select **OK**

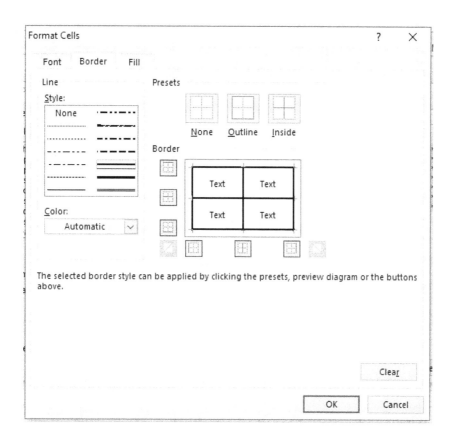

8) You will be taken back to New PivotTable Style dialog box. You can see a preview of what Pivot table design will look like in the

Preview section. Once you are happy, select **OK**

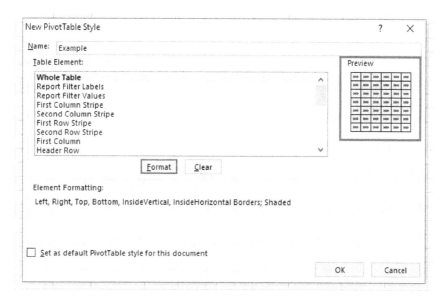

9) To apply this new custom pivot table style, click on **Design** tab in ribbon, and under **PivotTable Styles** group, click on down arrow to open up Pivot table styles

as explained in step 2. Your newly created pivot table style will be located under **Custom** heading. Click your left mouse button to apply your custom style to Pivot table

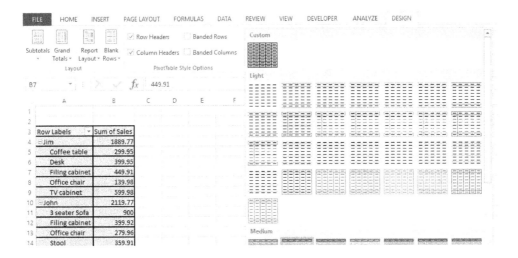

10) Repeat these steps to apply formatting to any other elements

Tip: If you want custom pivot table style to be default style, then just check **Choose as default style for document** box in Modify dialog Style box.

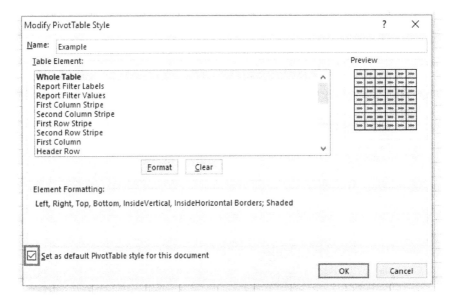

Pivot Table Style Options

You can apply further pivot table style options in **PivotTable Style Options** group. This is located in **Design** tab in ribbon.

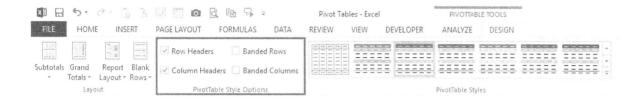

There are four options to choose from:

1) **Row Headers** – This adds or removes shading to row headers depending on whether you select this option or not

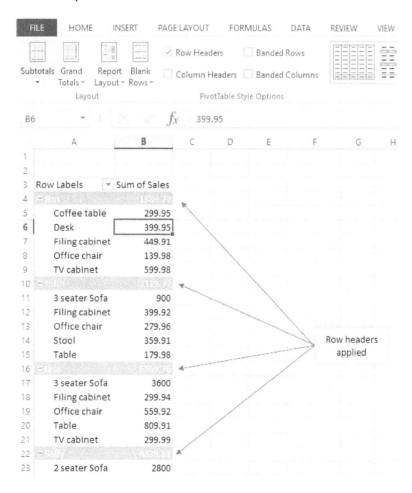

2) **Column Headers** – This adds or removes shading to column header depending on if this option is selected or not.

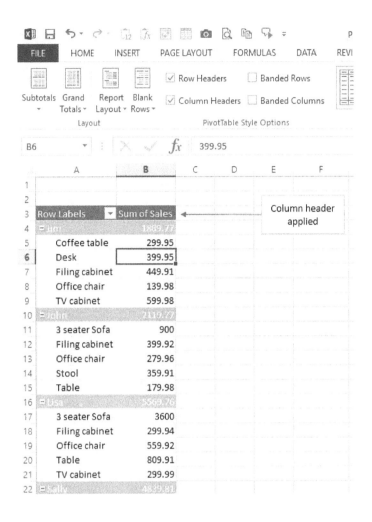

3) **Banded Rows** – If this option is selected, then it applies a thick line between each row

4) **Banded Columns** - If this option is selected, then it applies a thick line between each column

| B7 | ▾ | : | ✕ | ✓ | fx | 449.91 |

	A	B	C	D	E	F
1						
2						
3	Row Labels ▾	Sum of Sales				
4	⊟ Jim	1889.77				
5	Coffee table	299.95				
6	Desk	399.95				
7	Filing cabinet	449.91				
8	Office chair	139.98				
9	TV cabinet	599.98				
10	⊟ John	2119.77				
11	3 seater Sofa	900				
12	Filing cabinet	399.92				
13	Office chair	279.96				
14	Stool	359.91				
15	Table	179.98				
16	⊟ Lisa	5569.76				
17	3 seater Sofa	3600				
18	Filing cabinet	299.94				
19	Office chair	559.92				
20	Table	809.91				
21	TV cabinet	299.99				
22	⊟ Sally	4839.81				
23	2 seater Sofa	2800				

Applying Number Formatting

To make your pivot tables more meaningful, you can apply number formatting to values. For example, you can apply different currencies, decimal places, date formats, percentages, and so on. Pivot table I have created so far contains just values under Sales column. We don't know what these values actually mean. In this example, I will show you steps to change values to US dollars.

1) Select a cell in Pivot table and right-click mouse

2) From shortcut menu, select **Number Format**

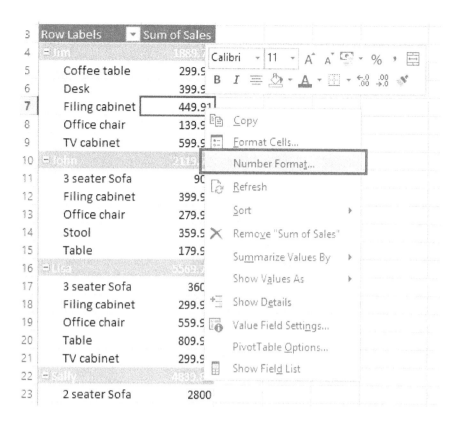

3) In Format Cells dialog box, select **Currency** under **Category**. Select a currency symbol from drop-down menu in **Symbol** field. In this example, I selected **$ English (United States)**. You can also choose how many decimal places you want in **Decimal Places** field. default is 2 decimal places, and in this example, I have left it at 2. Once you are happy with your selections, then press **OK** button.

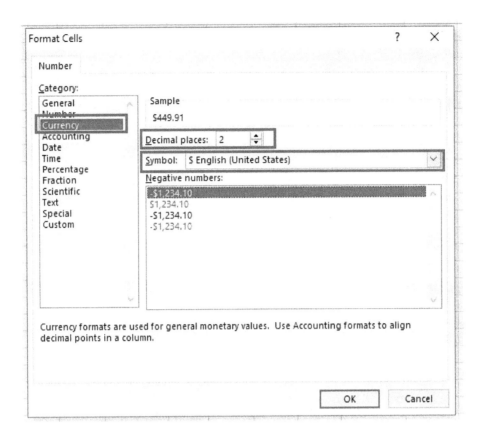

4) sales are now in US dollars

	A	B
1		
2		
3	Row Labels ▼	Sum of Sales
4	⊟ Jim	$1,889.77
5	Coffee table	$299.95
6	Desk	$399.95
7	Filing cabinet	$449.91
8	Office chair	$139.98
9	TV cabinet	$599.98
10	⊟ John	$2,119.77
11	3 seater Sofa	$900.00
12	Filing cabinet	$399.92
13	Office chair	$279.96
14	Stool	$359.91
15	Table	$179.98
16	⊟ Lisa	$5,569.76
17	3 seater Sofa	$3,600.00
18	Filing cabinet	$299.94
19	Office chair	$559.92
20	Table	$809.91
21	TV cabinet	$299.99
22	⊟ Sally	$4,839.81
23	2 seater Sofa	$2,800.00

Move Field Position in Pivot table Field Pane

You may want to change look of your pivot table, so it shows information in a different way. You can move fields up or down, so they are located in different positions. For example, Pivot table below shows what furniture each Sales person has sold and sales amount. Sales Person field is in first position, and Product field is in second position in Rows area of Pivot table Fields pane.

I now want to move Product field in first position in Rows area, so it is above Sales Person field. There are two ways to do this:

1) Clicking and dragging field and moving it to first position in Rows area. In this example, I would click and drag Product field and move it above Sales Person field

2) Clicking field and from shortcut menu select **Move up**. In this example, I would click Product field and select **Move up,** which will move field above Sales Person field

Notice dynamic of Pivot table has changed, and main row headers are furniture items and not Sales people.

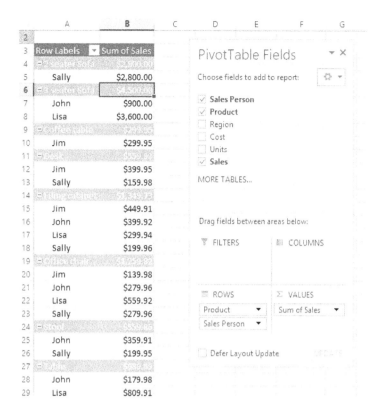

You can change field positions back again using same methods above.

Change Pivot Table Headings

You may want to give your pivot table headings more suitable names. By default, row headings are called 'Row Labels,' column headings are called 'Column Labels', and value headings start with 'Sum of' if calculation to summarise values is SUM. It would be called 'Count of' if calculation is count, 'Average of' if an average is used as calculation, and so on.

Row Labels	Sum of Sales
⊟ Jim	$1,889.77
Coffee table	$299.95
Desk	$399.95
Filing cabinet	$449.91
Office chair	$139.98
TV cabinet	$599.98
⊟ John	$2,119.77
3 seater Sofa	$900.00
Filing cabinet	$399.92
Office chair	$279.96
Stool	$359.91
Table	$179.98
⊟ Lisa	$5,569.76
3 seater Sofa	$3,600.00
Filing cabinet	$299.94
Office chair	$559.92
Table	$809.91
TV cabinet	$299.99
⊟ Sally	$4,839.81
2 seater Sofa	$2,800.00
Desk	$159.98
Filing cabinet	$199.96
Office chair	$279.96
Stool	$199.95

To change Pivot table's headings is simple. Just select Pivot table heading you want to change and, in Formula bar, type new heading name. In this example, I have named row heading 'Sales Person' and values heading 'Sales by Sales Person.'

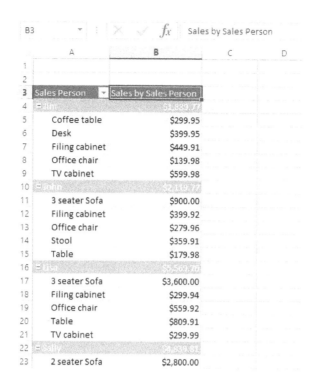

Tip: You cannot name Pivot table heading same name as a field name. For example, if I tried to name values heading 'Sales,' I would get following message because there is a field name in Values area already called 'Sales.'

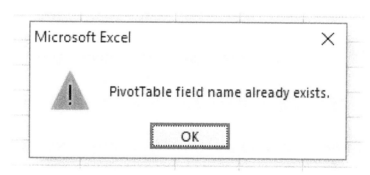

You can over-ride this by adding a space after heading name. Excel sees space as a character, so it will see heading and field name as two different names.

B3	× ✓ fx	Sales

	A	B
1		
2		
3	Sales Person ▾	Sales
4	⊟ Jim	$1,889.77
5	Coffee table	$299.95
6	Desk	$399.95
7	Filing cabinet	$449.91
8	Office chair	$139.98
9	TV cabinet	$599.98
10	⊟ John	$2,119.77
11	3 seater Sofa	$900.00
12	Filing cabinet	$399.92
13	Office chair	$279.96
14	Stool	$359.91
15	Table	$179.98
16	⊟ Lisa	$5,569.76
17	3 seater Sofa	$3,600.00
18	Filing cabinet	$299.94
19	Office chair	$559.92
20	Table	$809.91
21	TV cabinet	$299.99
22	⊟ Sally	$4,839.81
23	2 seater Sofa	$2,800.00

Chapter 6: - Skills To Know When Job Hunting

Excel Sorting Tasks for Job Searching

One of the most typical jobs you'll need to know while using Excel in your new profession is sorting a sequence of cells. If you take a pre-hire competency exam, you may be given a random collection of facts that you must arrange. Excel allows you to alphabetize a list of last names or order a sequence of numbers from highest to lowest with a single click of a button. Words and numbers can also be sorted in the same way, from lowest to highest or vice versa.

Another option for sorting your data is to copy and paste information from its current cell to the area where you truly need it. If you've ever used a copy and paste feature in another software, you'll know how to utilize the one in Excel. To paste, select a cell and press Ctrl + C (or Ctrl + X to cut it), then select the desired destination cell and press Ctrl + V. If you wish to copy a whole row, column, or group of cells, use this method. Select your preferred cells by clicking the row number on the left side of the window, the column letter on the top of the window, or by using your mouse to highlight them, then use the copy and paste procedures described previously.

The Hide and Unhide options in Excel provide the last choice for sorting. This allows you to hide a row or column from view while keeping the data in the spreadsheet intact. You may conceal a row or column by right-clicking the row number or column letter, then selecting Conceal. To reveal a hidden row or column, pick the rows or columns immediately before and follow the hidden series using your mouse.

Formatting Options

Another category of Excel activities that you may regularly encounter centers on modifying the appearance and printing of your cells. You may change the color of your cells, the look of the font, and the size of your cells in each version of Excel. Color changes may be made easily in all versions of Excel by right-clicking the cell and selecting one of the formatting choices from the shortcut menu.

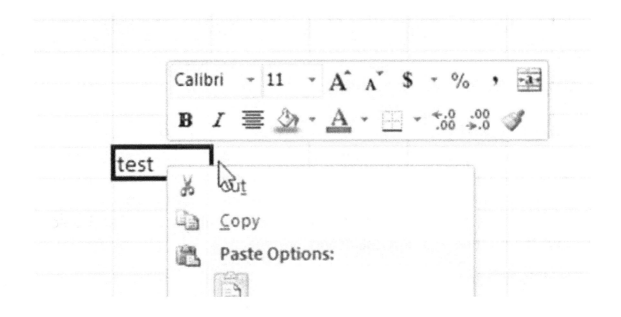

Right-click on the row number or column name and pick row height or column width. If you pick a group of rows or columns, the same function is used.

The Page Setup menu provides the last option for formatting the look of your Excel file, particularly for printing. Click the Page Setup button in the bottom-right corner of the Page Setup section on the Page Layout menu to access the Page Setup menu.

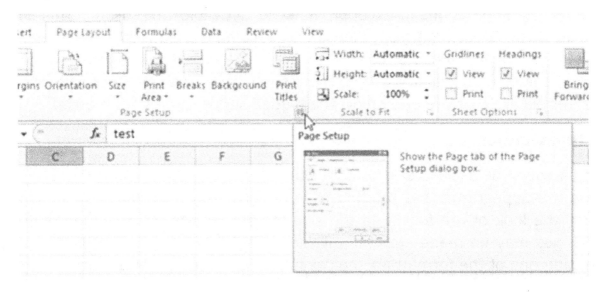

This menu lets you choose the orientation of your page, page margins, header information, and whether or not gridlines should be printed on the page. Printing gridlines is an extremely important factor when printing Excel files since it provides the best method for making a printed document more legible. Unless otherwise told, I generally include these by default.

Practice & Practice

Excel, like nearly everything else in life, requires practice to improve. You may execute certain activities with guidance. Still, your true worth to a potential employer will emerge when you can complete any of these duties smoothly from memory. This will enhance your production, which will raise your worth. Furthermore, as you continue to use Excel, you will discover new approaches to do jobs. You will also discover additional useful tips and methods for quickly organizing, sorting, and manipulating huge volumes of data.

If you're just starting in the job market or wanting to change careers, you've undoubtedly noticed that many of the available positions demand some level of computer knowledge. The exact amount of the required abilities may vary greatly depending on the sort of work you seek. Still, even the most basic occupations that need you to sit in front of a computer will require some understanding of Microsoft Excel. However, this job need should not be a total obstacle if you are inexperienced with the program. You may use this section to understand what you need to know about Microsoft Excel before applying for jobs that need it.

Become acquainted with the Excel interface and terminology.

Many organizations still use Microsoft Excel 2003, which may surprise you. Companies have a propensity to wait until an issue arises before making adjustments or updates to their system. Since then, there have been two complete version upgrades, yet Excel still has a sizable user base. So, while applying for a job, you may need to know multiple Excel versions. However, regardless of whatever version of Microsoft Excel you're using (new versions are produced every few years and are recognized by their release year), A few items will always remain the same in Microsoft Excel 2010 (for example). A pattern of tiny rectangles covers the bulk of the Excel display. Each of these rectangles represents a cell, which is arranged into rows and columns. A row is a horizontal succession of cells, whereas a column is a vertical sequence of cells.

When you click on one of the cells, you may input a number or letter appearing in the cell. The value is the information in the cell.

Using the options at the top of the screen, you may arrange, sort, and change the look of your cells and values.

The menus will look different depending on the version of Excel you're using, and many different organizations, regrettably, utilize various versions of the application. However, the most fundamental functionality is there in each iteration, so as long as you know what you need to accomplish, you should be able to find the appropriate menu option.

Workbooks in Excel

A Microsoft Excel file collects worksheets, charts, graphs, and other relevant Excel objects into a single location. Workbooks come in various shapes and sizes, depending on the version of Microsoft Excel you're using. Each workbook has a distinct purpose that distinguishes it from the others.

What Are the Different Components of a Workbook?

Worksheets, which Excel users can use to store, edit, and manipulate data, charts, and graphs, which Excel users can use to display their data in a variety of customizable ways, and macros, which Excel users can use to create or record custom commands to fit their specific needs, are just a few of the components.

What Characteristics Does a Workbook Possess?

They include various functions, including the ability to create, rename, and modify numerous spreadsheets, charts, and graphs. They also give users the option of storing custom menus and instructions within each worksheet. Excel users may modify an Excel workbook in various ways using some of the most common features, such as macros, the ribbon, and the quick access toolbar.

What Are Workbook Tools Available?

Within Excel spreadsheets, users have access to a variety of essential features. Users may modify virtually any property using tools like the file menu and backstage view. Users may generate easy-to-access pictures of critical portions of their workbook using tools like custom views and frozen panes. Users can transmit and receive data from a variety of workbook-related sites using tools like exporting and importing.

What are the different kinds of Excel Workbooks?

There are several varieties of workbooks and numerous ways to export workbooks to other file formats. There are just too many varieties to discuss here. But I'll make an exception. For a good reason, the Excel Workbook is one of the most widely used workbooks. This worksheet can be opened in most versions of Excel-by-Excel users.

Is it possible to protect my workbook?

Yes, you can secure a workbook in Excel in a few different ways. Password encryption and worksheet and workbook protection are just a few features that help users secure their workbooks. Other users won't be able to quickly modify the appearance and format of your workbook if you utilize tools like concealing worksheets and marking it as final. Depending on the situation, users can construct custom views and freeze panes to show or conceal particular views. These are especially useful when your workbooks get larger, and you need to condense material in various ways.

Work 30 mins / Day

You've probably heard the phrase "work smarter, not harder". If you need to improve your productivity and work habits in Excel, make sure you're working in Excel! The Excel spreadsheet is a powerful tool. Using it well can help you become more productive and efficient in your work. You'll learn how to create a never-ending list of activities for yourself that will keep productivity consistently high and avoid the traps that prevent many people from succeeding at their jobs. By applying the principles, you will learn here, I guarantee that you will exceed your previous productivity levels.

Balance Examples

Excel is a great tool for keeping track of your finances, whether you are budgeting for the entire month or managing your investments. You can also use it to realistically estimate what your future expenses might be, by using something called 'cash flow'.

Cash flow is used by all sorts of business owners and people who invest their money. It is a way of forecasting what your expenses will be in the future, based on how much money you have right at the time of figuring out your cash flow.

Excel's cash flow can be used in a variety of ways. You can project your expected income and expenses using basic formulas that use numbers from your bank statement, or you can create a more complicated model by creating charts from your bank statement data, and then plugging in numbers from your projected cash flow.

Chapter 8: - Common Errors

Printing Difficulties

This is also a bug that is often found. When a user tries to print from a specific region inside a spreadsheet, it generates a page break for each and every cell, including the user's best efforts to fit the collection into one page. And it gives a margin error any time a user tries to scale the image.

Well, this is a really inconvenient problem, so learn about the most popular causes and how to fix the Excel printing mistake.

Causes include:

- It has been discovered that the problem arises as a result of the following circumstances:

- The printer driver has been corrupted.

- Alternatively, the customer does not have a default printer driver installed.

Resolution:

To resolve the problem, it is suggested that the printer driver be updated and that a new printer driver be used as the default printer driver. To do so, obey these instructions:

- To begin, open the Add Printer dialogue box as follows:

- Select Add a printer from the drop-down menu.

- Select Add a local printer from the Add Printer box.

- And then select Use an existing port, then Next.

- Now, select Microsoft from the Manufacturer drop-down menu.

- Next, select Microsoft XPS Document Writer.

- After that, select Use the currently configured driver (recommended) > Next.

- Pick Set as the default printer from the drop-down menu, then clicks Next.

- Finally, press the Finish button.

Verify that changing printer drivers resolves the problem:

- Excel can be used to open the spreadsheet.

- Select *File* > Print from the drop-down menu, then press the Print button.

- Found Unreadable Content

This is a typical Excel error that users encounter when they try to open an XlsxWriter file and receive the following message:

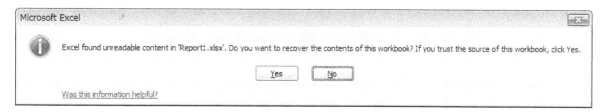

This challenging error in Excel's default alert about any validation error in XML used for the elements of the XLSX file, it is realized that the text is unreadable error is caused by the corruption of the whole Excel file or the corruption of one or more objects in the Excel file.

However, there are several manual methods that may assist in the correction of Excel errors. To obey all of the corrections,

Added formulas Performance Problems:

Excel users have complained about the slow performance. In XLSX Excel formats, formulas with a connection to an entire column may cause performance issues. In particular, formulas that reference an entire column in XLSX Excel formats can create performance issues.

This is due to the expanded column size of the most recent Excel..

Users must adjust the slow-calculating worksheets in Excel to make them compute tens, hundreds, or maybe even thousands of times quicker. To do so, switch the calculation modes from automated to manual. This will help you prevent the Excel output issues caused by added formulas.

Pasting Error

Excel pasting error is a very annoying error that consumers encounter from time to time when pasting details/data from one Excel document to another.

This mistake isn't exclusive to one Excel text, but it affects a number of them. "The details you are attempting to paste do not fit the cell type (Currency, Text, Date, or other formats) for the cells in the column," says the error message.

The primary cause of the mistake is yet to be determined. However, to correct the Excel error of being unable to paste results, use the following solution:

- If you're attempting to paste a vast volume of data, make sure the cell structure for the cells in the column fits the structure of the data you're pasting, and then paste the data one column at a time.

- You may also fix the error by changing the cell format for a column.

- To do so, follow these steps:

- First, press the column heading for the column that needs to be changed (A, B, C, and so on).

- Then, on the *Home* page, choose Number Format from the drop-down menu.

- After that, choose the cell format that corresponds to the data you're trying to paste into the column.

They hope that the provided solutions will assist you in resolving popular Excel errors; however, if the error persists despite following the provided solutions, please contact us. In this scenario, use the automatic Excel problem-solving approach to quickly get back to work on your Excel application.

Copy the Formula

To easily copy a formula, use the following steps:

- Hovering over a cell with the formula in the bottom-right corner (one will see that the pointer has become a thick black +)

- Press the black + sign twice.

- Taking formulas or Values and Pasting Them • If this technique doesn't fit because the range starts at a blank cell and ends at a blank cell, or one does not want to pull a formula down to Thousand rows, do this instead: • Select the first cell one want to copy or fill in with data.

- In the name box, write the address of the last cell in the range where one wants to enter the data or the formula, then press Shift + Enter.

- To modify the formula in the first cell, press F2.

- Finally, press CTRL + Enter.

IFERROR

When the formula produces a mistake, the Excel IFERROR feature returns a custom outcome, and when no error is found, it returns a normal result. IFERROR is a simple way to catch and handle errors without the need for nested IF statements.

Formula: =IFERROR (value, value if error)

Parameters:

Value represents the error detection value, algorithm, or reference.

Value if error is the value of the outcome if an error is present.

When an error in a calculation is identified, the IFERROR algorithm returns an alternate solution or formula.

The IFERROR module can be used to identify and manage errors caused by other functions or formulas. IFERROR identifies the subsequent error messages: #REF!, #DIV/0!, #VALUE!, #NUM!, #NULL! Or #NAME?

If A1 includes the number 10, B1 is empty, and C1 contains the formula =A1/B1, this IFERROR will catch the error #DIV/0 caused by dividing A1/B1.

C1 will display the message "Please enter a value in B1" if B1 is null or void and B1 is empty. Upon receiving a number in cell B1, the formula would return the product of A1/B1.

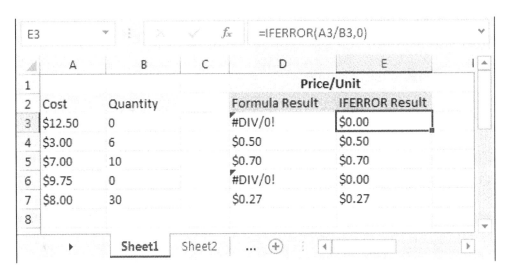

IFNA

When the formula produces a #N/A error, the IFNA function displays the customized result, and when no mistake is found, it returns a normal outcome.

IFNA is a clever way to capture and treat #N/A error when ignoring any other errors.

Formula: =IFNA (value, value_if_na)

Parameters:

Value is The value or algorithm, or reference that would be used to look for errors.

Value if na is if there is a #N/A mistake, this will be the value to be returned. The following is an illustration of IFNA being used to capture #N/A errors with VLOOKUP: =IFNA (VLOOKUP(A1,table,2,0),"Not found")

As a value is blank, it is treated as a blank string ("") rather than a mistake.

If value if na is set to a blank string (""), when a mistake occurs, no message is shown.

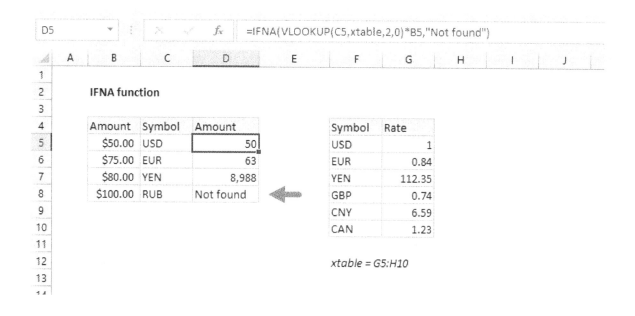

Formulas Not Working

It's possible that when one confirms a formula (by pressing enter), the answer doesn't appear; rather, The formula is shown in the cell.

The Solution is The issue is that the cell is formatted as text, so Excel interprets the formula as text.

Simply transform the cell to a Number/ General format, then verify the formula.

Formula View

This occurs more often by chance when the spreadsheet displays all calculations but not their output.

	1	=C4+1	=D4+1
Sales	100	200	250
Commission	=C5*10%	=D5*10%	=E5*10%

The entire spreadsheet is showing formulas & not the result

The Solution is to Simply click CTRL ~ again to return to regular mode.

Hashes in the Cell

Sometimes the cells would be loaded up with hashes. This may be because the cell data does not fit in the cell's width. The data is in excess of 253 letters A -ve number in the cell has been configured as a Date or Time format. Note the date or time must be positive numbers. The Fix is to Widen the column's width. For autofit, Shortcut is ALT OCA, or ALT OCW is for specific custom width) Reduce the no of characters in the cell value.

Please ensure the cell does not have a -ve number that is formatted as the date or time.

Page Breaks

Page breaks are innocuous, and they make the spreadsheet untidy.

The Solution is to Go to Options, then to Advanced, then to Scroll down to look for displaying options for the current spreadsheet, then untick Page Breaks

Excel Security

It is possible to apply encryption to Excel spreadsheets, but it is riddled with issues. The focus of protection is on the spreadsheet's configuration rather than the details. One may attempt to lock certain sheets and cells to prevent users from modifying the layout & formula, but they can generally alter any of it if they see the data.

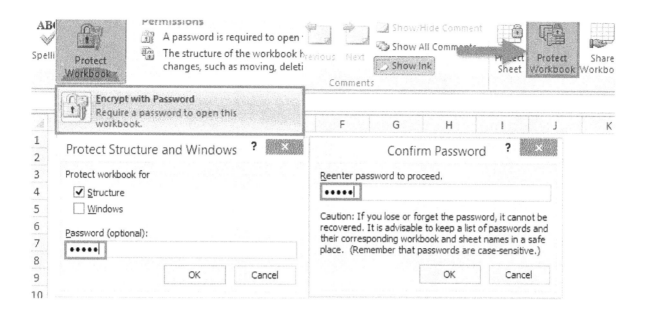

Switch the Enter key's influence. Excel shifts to the next down cell as one presses the Enter key. But what if one prefers to sit in the same cell? By using Tools, then Options, then Edit, one can make the Enter key carry them in either direction or keep them in the same cell.

Final Words

Excel is completely equipped with robust features that enable it to satisfy the needs of all users, whether for academic or corporate objectives. This Microsoft office application's user-friendliness has remained unchanged despite the addition of new features that enhance its already impressive capability.

What are the most significant benefits of using Microsoft Excel?

Without Microsoft Excel, organizing and comparing data would be time-consuming and frustrating. It allows users to efficiently construct, maintain, and compare lists. In addition, this application's spreadsheet structure makes it simple to segregate rows and columns of data.

Excel is a user-friendly tool that simplifies and streamlines activities, whether you're working with business financial data or managing your personal checkbook. Additionally, Microsoft Excel can be used to complete arithmetic homework, construct mailing lists, and organize book, music, and video collections. It can also be used to assist with family budgeting.

What are the advantages of utilizing this program?

Calculating is a piece of cake using Excel. The application automatically computes the mean, sum, difference, and product of a series of numbers. In addition, it features functions capable of handling more intricate financial calculations and data. It is also applicable for comparing logical statements.

Data analysis is among the additional functions. It is possible to sort, filter, and import data, as well as generate graphs and pivot tables. It also contains numerous formatting and customisation features. It is not even difficult to work on many spreadsheets simultaneously. Excel can create and managing many sheets within a single worksheet.

What are the most frequent uses for Microsoft Excel? Excel has an abundance of useful functions. The bulk of users, however, construct personal databases. Excel is designed to make data collection, organizing, and analysis simple and straightforward. Since Excel permits the construction of grids and charts, data can be analyzed further. Excel also makes calculations straightforward, regardless of the amount of data involved. Therefore, it is suitable for business reporting.

Other Microsoft Excel applications include inventory management, budgeting, and profit breakeven analysis. Excel is not only useful for corporate purposes, but also for homemakers and students.

www.ingramcontent.com/pod-product-compliance
Lightning Source LLC
Chambersburg PA
CBHW060200060326
40690CB00018B/4184